FALAFEL

FALAFEL

DELICIOUS RECIPES FOR MIDDLE EASTERN-STYLE PATTIES, PLUS SAUCES, PICKLES, SALADS & BREADS

WITH RECIPES BY
DUNJA GULIN

RYLAND PETERS & SMALL
LONDON • NEW YORK

Designer Geoff Borin
Creative Director Leslie Harrington
Senior Editor Abi Waters
Editorial Director Julia Charles
Production Manager Gordana Simakovic

Indexer Vanessa Bird

First published in 2023 by
Ryland Peters & Small
20–21 Jockey's Fields   341 E 116th St
London WC1R 4BW   New York, NY 10029

www.rylandpeters.com

10 9 8 7 6 5 4 3 2 1

Text © Dunja Gulin, plus Ghillie Basan, Matt Follas,
Kathy Kordalis, Theo A. Michaels, Hannah Miles,
Louise Pickford, Claire Power, Leah Vanderveldt,
Laura Washburn Hutton and Sarah Wilkinson 2023

Design and photographs © Ryland Peters & Small
2023

See page 160 for full credits.

Recipes in this book by Dunja Gulin have previously
been published by Ryland Peters & Small in *Falafel
Forever*, *Tahini*, *Hummus is Where the Heart Is* and *The
Gut Health Cookbook*.

ISBN: 978-1-78879-527-2

A CIP record for this book is available from the
British Library. US Library of Congress cataloguing-
in-publication data has been applied for.

Printed in China

Notes

· Both British (Metric) and American (Imperial
plus US cups) measurements are included in
these recipes for your convenience; however it is
important to work with one set of measurements
and not alternate between the two when
following a recipe.

· All spoon measurements are level unless
otherwise specified. A teaspoon is 5 ml and
a tablespoon is 15 ml.

· Ovens should be preheated to the specified
temperature. Recipes in this book were tested
using a regular oven. If using a fan-assisted/
convection oven, follow the manufacturer's
instructions for adjusting temperatures.

· When a recipe calls for the grated zest of citrus
fruit, buy unwaxed fruit and wash well before
using. If you can only find treated fruit, scrub
well in warm soapy water before using.

· Always use sterilized jars. For more information
visit the Food Standards Agency (FSA) website
in the UK or the United States Department of
Agriculture (USDA) website in the US.

· Everyone's hummus intake is different, but for
this book we have assumed an approximate
serving amount of 50 g/2 oz. hummus for one
small serving or 100 g/3½ oz. for one large
serving per person.

CONTENTS

INTRODUCTION

Growing up, I'd never heard of falafel, let alone eaten it or seen it being prepared – it's not something you would find on the streets of the small town in Istria, Croatia, where I was raised in the 1980s. However, all the ingredients were readily available and could be frequently found in the kitchens of my grandmas and my parents; chickpeas/garbanzo beans were a staple, especially in stews and for salads. Actually, my grandma has been cultivating chickpeas/garbanzo beans since the 1960s and, even today, each time I visit her I know that a huge bag of them will be waiting for me on my way out!

It wasn't until the late 1990s, when I moved to London as a young foodie on a mission to discover new tastes, that I first saw and tasted falafel. I clearly remember that Saturday in Shepherd's Bush Market when a falafel stall caught my attention. I had no smartphone to take me to a good vegetarian restaurant and there were no website reviews telling me what's tasty and what's not – looking for food in a big city was a totally different experience back then! I asked the vendor a couple of questions, and as soon as I heard the word 'chickpeas', I knew that was it! The wrap I bought was like nothing I had tasted before – warm fritters wrapped in pitta bread with just the right balance of creaminess and tanginess from the hummus and the pickles and the added veggies.

Wow! It wasn't long before I copied a falafel recipe from a Middle Eastern cookbook in a bookstore, and I have been making my own falafel ever since.

My grandma's chickpeas/garbanzo beans are still the most important ingredient to me when making falafel. However, over time, I have experimented with many other ingredients that can be used to make alternative falafel-like dishes. This means that people who don't like fried foods, or who find traditional falafel difficult to digest, or even those who are following a raw food diet, don't have to miss out on enjoying a good falafel-like meal.

I sincerely hope you will like my selection of fried, baked and raw falafels and everything that goes well with them from hummus to pickles to pitta breads. Enjoy!

TIPS & TRICKS

I make all kinds of falafels, and I find that when people try them or see a photo the questions usually start popping up: How come they aren't falling apart or soaking up all the oil? How do I achieve the fine crust and the juicy inside? What is the secret ingredient that makes them so tasty? These, along with many other questions, reveals that making really good falafel can be a tricky business. Now that I think of it, there are a couple of crucial moments where a small mistake can make the difference between a perfect falafel and a falafel mix that ends up being thrown away! So, dear foodie friends, it is my duty to reveal all my tips and tricks, and I sincerely hope you find these instructions helpful.

• When making falafel with soaked chickpeas/garbanzo beans, make sure they are soaked for at least 24 hours. Not only will the 24-hour soak make them softer and easier to blend, but the falafel will be easier to digest and you'll feel lighter and more nourished after a falafel meal.

• When making cooked grain-based and bean-based falafel, if using leftover grains and beans, make sure they are at room temperature, not fridge-cold.

• When vegetables are part of the falafel mix, chop them or grate them finely. Otherwise, bigger pieces might cause the mix to fall apart during frying.

• Mix well, or even knead the falafel mixture for a while, until all the ingredients are well combined.

• For deep-fried falafel, never use bread crumbs to bind the mixture if it seems wet – your falafel will fall apart and soak up loads of oil. This rule is for deep-fried falafel only; for shallow-frying or baking, adding bread crumbs to the mix is okay.

• Most falafel mixes have to sit for at least half an hour to bind well.

• Use a small heavy-bottomed stainless-steel or cast-iron pan/ skillet for frying.

• Falafels made from soaked chickpeas/garbanzo beans or lentils need to fry for longer than falafels made from cooked grains or beans in order to be cooked properly.

• Add enough oil to the pan for deep-frying (at least 3 fingers up from the bottom of the saucepan).

• Heat the oil until it starts 'moving' – the right temperature of the frying oil is really important. If the oil isn't hot enough, the falafel will sink, soak up loads of oil and start falling apart. If, on the other hand, the oil is too hot, the falafel will burn from the outside and stay uncooked on the inside.

• Once you place a couple of falafels in the pan, the oil should immediately sizzle and foam. If this does not happen, you need to preheat the oil a bit more.

• Overcrowding the pan will result in a dramatic drop in oil temperature and this will cause the falafel to fall apart and/or turn oily and remain uncooked. How many to cook at once depends on the size of your pan, but there should always be some free space left.

• If you're making a big batch of falafels that are rolled into flour or seeds, you'll probably, at some point, need to filter the oil through a steel sieve/strainer to remove burnt flour and food particles. These would, otherwise, spoil the taste and make the last batch taste bitter and burnt.

• Once the falafels are well browned (it is especially important to well-fry falafels that are made with soaked beans), use a skimmer to take them out and place them on a paper towel-lined plate. The oil mark on the towel should be small and not widely spread around your falafel. They should be compact, with a thin crust and a juicy inside, and should only lightly grease your fingers.

• Uncooked falafel mix made with soaked chickpeas/garbanzo beans can be frozen, and so can formed, uncooked falafel and already-fried leftover falafel. My advice is to fry the entire amount, and then freeze the leftovers. This way you only need to defrost them, drizzle some oil over and bake in the oven until crispy. They taste almost better than freshly fried falafel!

COOKING CHICKPEAS

The first thing you have to do to make a good hummus is cook the chickpeas/garbanzo beans well, so that they are soft, easier to digest and can be made into a creamy paste. I cook mine from scratch – it's a cheaper and healthier option than using canned ones, and the resulting hummus is divine. Dried chickpeas and beans need to be soaked for at least 12 hours before cooking. This step cannot be skipped as you could have stomach-ache and bloating if they aren't soaked and cooked properly.

180 g/1 cup chickpeas/garbanzo beans or other hard beans

1.9 litres/8 cups water, for soaking

700 ml/3 cups water, or more if needed, for cooking

2 dried bay leaves

5-cm/2-inch piece of kombu seaweed (optional)

PRESSURE-COOKING

I prefer to use a stove-top pressure cooker for cooking beans, since it's easy, doesn't require constant attention and beans cooked this way are softer and easier to digest. You do not need to have an expensive type of pressure cooker with a fancy lid that no one knows how to put together; there are inexpensive, mechanical, Italian-style models available, which will serve you for decades!

Soak the chickpeas or other beans in the soaking water for 12 hours. Drain, add to the pressure cooker, cover with the fresh water for cooking and bring to the boil. Drain, rinse well and cover again with fresh water, 3–4 cm/1¼–1½ inches above the level of chickpeas or beans. Add the bay leaves and kombu (if using). Secure the lid and allow to boil over a medium heat until it starts hissing and the pressure valve comes up. Reduce the heat to low (just enough to hear a low hissing sound of the steam coming out of the valve), and cook for 1 hour. Turn off the heat, allow the pressure to drop and open the lid.

The chickpeas or beans should be soft. If not using immediately, let cool, place in a glass container with a tight lid covered in cooking water and keep refrigerated. They can last for about 10 days.

BOILING

180 g/1 cup chickpeas/garbanzo beans or other hard beans

1.9 litres/8 cups water, for soaking

820 ml/3½ cups water, or more if needed, for cooking

2 dried bay leaves

5-cm/2-inch piece of kombu seaweed(optional)

If you don't own a pressure cooker, you can cook chickpeas or other beans in a regular, heavy-bottomed pot by boiling them until soft. It usually takes longer than pressure-cooking, and the cooking time depends a lot on the type of beans used, their size and age – beans that are older are harder and need to be cooked for longer. Soak the chickpeas or other beans in the soaking water for 12 hours. Drain, cover with fresh water (enough to cover) and bring to the boil. Drain, rinse well and cover again with 820 ml/3½ cups of water for cooking. Add the bay leaves and kombu (if using). Let boil over a high heat, uncovered. With a slotted spoon, remove any foam that might appear. Lower the heat, cover and cook until tender; 1 hour or more. Check every 20 minutes and add more hot water if needed. The chickpeas or beans should be tender when done.

SHOCK METHOD

180 g/1 cup chickpeas/garbanzo beans or other hard beans

1.9 litres/8 cups water, for soaking

600 ml/2½ cups water, plus more cold water for topping up, for cooking

2 dried bay leaves

5-cm/2-inch piece of kombu seaweed (optional)

This method is a bit more demanding and requires constant attention. You have to keep adding cold water during the cooking process, 'shocking' the hot beans to make their skins softer and easier to digest. The best type of pot to use is a heavy, cast-iron pot with a 'drop' lid that fits inside the pot. Beans cooked this way are sweeter-tasting and delicious.

Soak the chickpeas or other beans in the water for soaking for 12 hours. Drain, cover with fresh water (enough to cover) and let boil. Drain, rinse well and cover with the 600 ml/2½ cups of fresh water. Add the bay leaves and kombu (if using). Let boil over a medium heat, uncovered. With a slotted spoon, remove any foam that might appear. Lower the heat and float a lid that is smaller than the diameter of the saucepan on top of the beans. Keep an eye on the water level, removing the lid and adding more cold water down the side each time the water level becomes low. Continue cooking until they are tender; 1–2 hours.

FRIED FALAFELS

Surely you have tasted, or maybe even prepared, one version of this classic falafel recipe. An intensive 24-hour soak makes the chickpeas properly soft, which gives a lovely moist yet light mixture that is easy to digest.

TRADITIONAL CHICKPEA FALAFEL POCKETS

180 g/1 cup dried chickpeas/ garbanzo beans

80 g/⅔ cup chopped onion

2 garlic cloves

bunch of fresh parsley, leaves only

2 teaspoons ground coriander

½ teaspoon bicarbonate of soda/ baking soda

1 teaspoon ground cumin

⅛ teaspoon chilli/chili powder

1½ teaspoons salt

230 ml/1 cup oil, for frying

SERVING SUGGESTION

4 pitta pockets

Tahini Sauce (see page 113)

raw vegetables (such as sliced tomatoes, cucumber, lettuce, radishes, parsley, spring onions/ scallions)

MAKES 24–26 SMALL FALAFELS

Soak the chickpeas in plenty of water for 12 hours. Drain, discarding the water, cover with fresh water and let soak for another 12 hours. Drain, rinse well and let drain again for another 5 minutes.

It's best to use a food processor fitted with an 'S' blade for blending the falafel mix, even though it can also be done in a good blender, in 2 batches.

First blend the drained chickpeas; the texture should resemble coarse sand. Add all the remaining ingredients (except the frying oil) and blend until you get a paste. Cover with clingfilm/plastic wrap and let sit in the fridge for 1 hour, or longer.

Roll into walnut-sized balls, wetting your hands once in a while to prevent sticking.

Deep-fry the falafels in hot oil for 4 minutes or until nicely browned (see tips page 9). Because we're using soaked chickpeas, these falafels need to be deep-fried to make them digestible – baking them wouldn't work.

Warm the pitta pockets, fill with vegetables of your choice, add falafel balls and serve with the tahini sauce. Yum!

The most important step in making this falafel is to blend all the ingredients really well into a thick paste. Chunky falafel mix burns easily and tends to fall apart during frying – we want these pointed falafels to get a nice crunchy crust with a juicy, bright-green inside. You can use fresh or thawed peas instead of broad/fava beans, with equally yummy results.

FRESH BROAD BEAN FALAFEL

350 g/2⅓ cups shelled fresh broad/fava beans

2 garlic cloves, crushed

½ small bunch fresh mint, leaves only

½ small bunch fresh parsley, leaves only

½ teaspoon salt

¼ teaspoon cumin seeds, crushed

1 teaspoon ground coriander

1 tablespoon gram flour (chickpea/garbanzo bean flour)

230 ml/1 cup oil, for frying

SERVING SUGGESTION
baked pumpkin squares
pink or regular sauerkraut
rocket/arugula or microgreens
Cashew 'Yogurt' Sauce or Tofu Mayonnaise (see page 106)

MAKES 10 FALAFELS

Bring a pan of water to the boil and boil the broad beans for 1 minute. Drain and run them under cold water to cool them down to the point where you can handle them. Pinch their skins off with your fingers and slip the inner bright green beans out. You should get about 250 g/1½ cups peeled beans.

In a food processor fitted with an 'S' blade, chop the mint and parsley leaves, then add the skinned beans and whiz until chopped into a paste. Scoop into a bowl, add the remaining ingredients (except the frying oil) and knead for a second to incorporate.

Scoop up small amounts of mixture and use 2 spoons to shape into oval balls with lightly pointed ends. Deep-fry in hot oil for 3–4 minutes or until nicely browned (see tips page 9).

I serve these falafels in wide bowls, placed alongside baked pumpkin, pink sauerkraut and rocket, and drizzled with cashew 'yogurt' sauce or tofu mayo. A very satisfying and nutritious meal!

Chickpeas/garbanzo beans aren't the only legumes you can soak to make falafel! Red lentils are also an option – they make a falafel that is softer and easier to digest, and the soaking time is shorter! I usually add Indian spices to the mix, as well as young chard greens from my garden, but feel free to use any spices and any type of soft greens you can lay your hands on!

RED LENTIL FALAFEL WRAPS

90 g/½ cup split red lentils

40 g/1 cup finely chopped chard or spinach

2 garlic cloves

½ teaspoon salt

1 teaspoon finely chopped fresh ginger

1 teaspoon curry powder

½ teaspoon ground coriander

½ teaspoon ground turmeric

½ teaspoon garam masala

½ teaspoon ground ginger

⅛ teaspoon chilli/chili powder (or to taste)

230 ml/1 cup oil, for frying

SERVING SUGGESTION

wholegrain tortillas

young lettuce leaves

Super Simple Salsa (see page 109)

Herb & Avocado Dip (see page 108)

MAKES 12 FALAFELS

Wash the red lentils thoroughly and let them soak in plenty of water overnight. Drain, rinse well and let drain again for 5 minutes. It's best to use a food processor fitted with an 'S' blade for blending the falafel mix, even though it can also be done in a good blender. Blend all the ingredients (except the frying oil) until you get a paste – the texture should resemble coarse sand.

Roll into walnut-sized balls, then pat them down just a little to get chubby oval-shaped falafels. To prevent sticking, wet your hands while shaping.

Deep-fry the falafels in hot oil for 4 minutes or until nicely browned (see tips page 9). Because we're using soaked lentils, these falafels need to be deep-fried to make them digestible – baking them wouldn't work.

To assemble, warm the tortillas in the oven, add some lettuce and 4 or 5 falafels on top of each one, together with 2 tablespoons each of salsa and avocado dip. Wrap up and serve with extra dips. Or, even better, put all the ingredients on the table and let everyone make their own wraps!

This is a falafel recipe with a slightly different spice twist! The fennel taste from the seeds and the bulb itself pair well with the refreshing citrus aroma from the lemon zest. A must-try!

FENNEL & LEMON-SCENTED FALAFEL

180 g/1 cup dried chickpeas/garbanzo beans

2 shallots

2 garlic cloves

½ bunch fresh fennel fronds or coriander/cilantro leaves

1 teaspoon fennel seeds, crushed

1 teaspoon grated lemon zest

½ teaspoon bicarbonate of soda/baking soda

1 teaspoon ground coriander

⅛ teaspoon chilli/chili powder

1½ teaspoons salt

230 ml/1 cup oil, for frying

SERVING SUGGESTION

pitta pockets

Romaine lettuce leaves

fennel bulb, shaved into thin shavings using a vegetable peeler

pickles

Tahini Sauce (see page 113, or other sauce of choice)

lemon wedges

MAKES 24–26 SMALL FALAFELS

Soak the chickpeas in plenty of water for 12 hours. Drain, discarding the water, cover with fresh water and let soak for another 12 hours. Drain, rinse well and let drain again for another 5 minutes. The 24-hour soak will make the falafel easier to digest and the mixture won't be too dry.

It's best to use a food processor fitted with an 'S' blade for blending the falafel mix, even though it can also be done in a good blender, in 2 batches.

First blend the drained chickpeas, the texture should resemble coarse sand. Add all the remaining ingredients (except the frying oil) and blend until you get a paste. Cover with clingfilm/plastic wrap and let sit in the fridge for 1 hour, or longer.

Roll into walnut-sized balls, wetting your hands once in a while to prevent sticking. Deep-fry the falafels in hot oil for 4 minutes until nicely browned (see page 9). Because we're using soaked chickpeas, these falafels need to be deep-fried to make them digestible – baking them wouldn't work.

Warm the pitta pockets and fill them with lettuce, fennel shavings, pickles and falafel balls, and serve with tahini sauce and lemon wedges.

If you're looking for an instant falafel recipe that requires minimal prep, check out these crunchy beauties! Serving them with a fair amount of sauce is key, since the use of gram flour (chickpea/garbanzo bean flour), instead of soaked chickpeas/garbanzo beans, results in a slightly drier consistency.

GRAM FLOUR & HARISSA PATTIES

120 g/1 cup gram flour (chickpea/garbanzo bean flour)

¼ teaspoon bicarbonate of soda/baking soda

½ teaspoon salt

½ teaspoon ground coriander

1 teaspoon harissa (or to taste)

¼ teaspoon dried oregano

30 g/1 tablespoon very finely chopped onion

80 ml/⅓ cup hot water

3 tablespoons coconut oil (or other oil), for frying

harissa paste and Tofu Mayonnaise (see page 106), to serve (optional)

MAKES 8–10 PATTIES

Combine the flour with the other dry ingredients, mix in the chopped onion and slowly start incorporating the hot water. You should get a non-sticky dough that can be shaped easily. Let the mixture sit for 10 minutes before forming it into small patties.

Heat the oil in a non-stick frying pan/skillet over a medium heat. Depending on the size of your pan you will need to fry them in at least 2 batches. Make sure not to overcrowd the pan. Lower the heat and let the falafels fry for 3–4 minutes on each side, or until golden brown. If you wish to build your spicy food tolerance, serve these with plenty of harissa paste, as well as tofu mayonnaise to cool!

I love tempeh, but it took me years to realize that the texture of it, when mashed, is absolutely perfect for falafel-style recipes! It binds together so well and doesn't absorb any oil during frying, which is kind of a big deal! Chilli flakes/hot pepper flakes add spiciness, and Kala Namak gives a very light egg-like aroma that non-vegans will appreciate.

ROBUST TEMPEH FAUX-LAFEL

300 g/2½ cups tempeh

70 g/½ cup finely chopped green (bell) pepper

3 tablespoons freshly chopped parsley or coriander/cilantro leaves

1 garlic clove, crushed

½ teaspoon isot Kurdish black pepper flakes (or other chilli flakes/hot red pepper flakes)

¾ teaspoon Kala Namak (black salt powder)

230 ml/1 cup oil, for frying

MAKES 10 LARGE OR 20 SMALL FALAFELS

Cover the whole piece of tempeh with boiling water in a pan and simmer for 15 minutes. This will make the tempeh softer, easier to digest and the falafel won't crumble (but you can skip cooking the tempeh if you're in a hurry). Drain, let cool a little, then mash with a fork.

Add all the other ingredients (except the frying oil) and mix, preferably with your hands, to form a compact dough.

Form the mixture into falafels (either 10 large ones or 20 small ones) and deep-fry in hot oil for 2–3 minutes or until golden brown (see tips page 9).

My favourite ways to serve these include: with pasta and tomato sauce in winter; or with vegan mayo, fresh tomato salsa and sliced avocado in summer.

How 'Greek-style' this courgette/zucchini falafel actually is I have no idea, but the courgette base, the chickpea/garbanzo bean addition and the yogurt-cucumber serving sauce made me think of one hot summer I spent in Greece a long time ago, enjoying amazing home-cooked food!

GREEK-STYLE FALAFEL FRITTERS

560 g/4 cups grated courgette/zucchini

1 teaspoon salt, plus extra to taste

4 tablespoons freshly chopped parsley leaves

¼ teaspoon ground turmeric

¼ teaspoon ground cumin

½ teaspoon ground coriander

80 g/½ cup gram flour (chickpea/garbanzo bean flour)

freshly ground black pepper

olive oil, for shallow frying

SERVING SUGGESTION
Tzatziki (see page 88)
lemon wedges
freshly chopped coriander/cilantro
flatbreads

MAKES 14–16 FRITTERS

Put the grated courgette in a bowl, add the 1 teaspoon salt, mix well and let sit for 10 minutes. Squeeze out most of the courgette juice and discard. Add the parsley, turmeric, cumin, coriander, flour, pepper and more salt to taste, then quickly mix with a spatula.

With the help of a small round cookie cutter or a measuring tablespoon, form 14–16 even-sized patties and flatten them down a bit.

Heat a non-stick frying pan/skillet over a medium heat, add a little olive oil and fry the falafels for 3–4 minutes on each side until golden brown.

Serve with tzatziki sauce, lemon wedges, coriander and flatbreads, or whichever way you like!

These falafels are crunchy on the outside and creamy on the inside, but make sure to serve them freshly fried! Kalamata olives can be omitted entirely or substituted with other types of olives, or even with chopped corn kernels, especially in summer. Tofu is rich in plant protein, has a mild taste and is an excellent occasional food for those of us who prefer plant-based meals that are light, yet nourishing.

CRUNCHY TOFU FAUX-LAFEL

280 g/1½ cups fresh firm tofu

90 g/½ cup Kalamata olives

2 tablespoons freshly chopped coriander/cilantro leaves or snipped chives

2 tablespoons gram flour (chickpea/garbanzo bean flour)

½ teaspoon ground turmeric

freshly ground black pepper

salt, if needed

230 ml/1 cup oil, for frying

SERVING SUGGESTION
roasted vegetables of your choice

vegan mayo or good-quality ketchup

MAKES 16–18 FALAFELS

In a food processor fitted with an 'S' blade, process the tofu until creamy. Transfer it into a mixing bowl.

Drain, pat dry and finely chop the Kalamata olives and add them to the tofu with the coriander or chives, gram flour, turmeric, pepper and salt. Combine well with a silicone spatula.

Roll into 16–18 even-sized balls, wetting your hands once in a while to prevent sticking. Deep-fry the falafels in hot oil for 2–3 minutes or until golden brown (see tips page 9).

Serve hot or warm with plenty of veggies, cooked and raw and with some vegan mayo or good-quality ketchup.

This falafel recipe uses rye flakes and millet – both ancient grains that are high in fibre and protein. Serve alongside the coriander/cilantro-feta pesto for the perfect snack.

GRAINY FALAFEL WITH CORIANDER-FETA PESTO

250 g/1½ cups dried chickpeas/garbanzo beans

40 g/scant ½ cup rye flakes, plus 3 tablespoons to finish

60 g/scant ⅓ cup millet, cooked and cooled

2 shallots, chopped

1 green chilli/chile, finely chopped

1 garlic clove, crushed

1 teaspoon each ground coriander, cumin and smoked paprika

½ teaspoon ground cinnamon

½ teaspoon chilli flakes/hot red pepper flakes

30 g/1 oz. coarsely chopped mixed flat-leaf parsley and coriander/cilantro

2 tablespoons rye flour

1 teaspoon bicarbonate of soda/baking soda

230 ml/1 cup oil, for frying

salt and freshly ground black pepper

Coriander-feta Pesto (see page 108), roasted red (bell) peppers and lime wedges, to serve

SERVES 4–6

Soak the chickpeas in plenty of water for 12 hours. Drain, discarding the water, cover with fresh water and let soak for another 12 hours. Drain, rinse well and let drain again for another 5 minutes. The 24-hour soak will make the falafel easier to digest and the mixture won't be too dry. It's best to use a food processor fitted with an 'S' blade for blending the falafel mix, even though it can also be done in a good blender, in two batches. First blend the drained chickpeas, the texture should resemble coarse sand.

Add the rye flakes, millet, shallots, green chilli, garlic, spices and herbs until a fine paste forms. Stir through the flour and bicarbonate of soda, and season to taste. Cover with clingfilm/plastic wrap and let sit in the fridge for 1 hour, or longer.

Roll into walnut-sized balls, wetting your hands once in a while to prevent sticking. Deep-fry the falafels in hot oil for 3–5 minutes or until nicely browned (see tips page 9). As we're using soaked chickpeas, these falafels need to be deep-fried to make them digestible – baking them wouldn't work.

Serve the falafel warm or at room temperature, plated with some Coriander-feta Pesto, roasted red (bell) pepper (if liked) and wedges of lime for squeezing.

BAKED FALAFELS

These millet-based croquettes still carry the distinct falafel flavour, with an added barbecue kick from the spice mix! Millet is a healthy grain, rich in iron and other nutrients, and if there are some cooked leftovers lying around in my fridge, I often use them to make these elegant croquettes. They are always well received, even by otherwise picky eaters!

BBQ FALAFEL CROQUETTES

100 g/½ cup millet

300 ml/1¼ cups boiling water

2 tablespoons finely chopped onion

1 teaspoon finely chopped garlic

1 teaspoon ground coriander

1½ teaspoons barbecue spice rub (with added salt)

6 g/¼ cup freshly chopped parsley leaves

80 g/¼ cup polenta/cornmeal

olive oil, for brushing

baking sheet, lined with baking parchment

MAKES 10 CROQUETTES

Wash and drain the millet well, then place in a saucepan and pour over the boiling water. Cover, lower the heat to a minimum and simmer for 12–15 minutes until the millet soaks up all the liquid and becomes soft. Spread on a plate to cool. (You can also use leftover cooked millet from previous meals, and skip this stage.)

Preheat the oven to 180°C (350°F) Gas 4.

Place the cooked millet in a large bowl and add the onion, garlic, spices and parsley. Knead well into a sticky dough that holds together.

Form 10 cylinder-shaped croquettes, brush each one with oil on all sides and roll them in the polenta. Transfer to the lined baking sheet and bake in the preheated oven for 15–20 minutes or until golden brown. They will brown nicely if you switch on the grill/broiler mode at the end of baking. Serve while warm.

This recipe was created in one of those moments when you really fancy a falafel meal but you don't really have the necessary ingredients... So you just take out all the leftovers from the fridge and trust your cooking experience to guide you through the creative process of birthing a new recipe! The result is sometimes, as in this case, a very tasty dish and a real keeper!

CHUNKY BAKED FALAFEL PATTIES

½ large onion (about 60 g/2 oz.)

2 garlic cloves

320 g/2 cups cooked red kidney beans, well drained

2 tablespoons toasted ground sesame seeds or ground flaxseeds/linseeds

1 tablespoon dark sesame oil (or pumpkin seed oil or olive oil)

1 teaspoon salt

2 tablespoons gram flour (chickpea/garbanzo bean flour)

¼ teaspoon bicarbonate of soda/baking soda

SERVING SUGGESTION
Roasted Red Pepper and Mustard Sauce (see page 110)

toasted sourdough

rocket/arugula

pickled vegetables of your choice

baking sheet, lined with baking parchment

MAKES 18 PATTIES

Preheat the oven to 180°C (350°F) Gas 4.

In a food processor fitted with an 'S' blade, finely chop the onion and garlic. Mash the beans with a fork, leaving some chunks, then mix the beans with the chopped vegetables and all the other ingredients. The mix should resemble a thick cookie dough. Use a measuring spoon to scoop 18 flat, free-form patties onto the lined baking sheet.

Bake in the preheated oven for 15–20 minutes until dry enough to remove from the baking sheet without falling apart.

These falafel patties are on the saltier side and I love them served on slices of freshly baked or just toasted sourdough bread with roasted red pepper and mustard sauce, rocket and any type of pickled vegetables on the side.

Note: you can use cooked chickpeas instead of kidney beans for a more traditional falafel flavour, if you like.

Baked falafels are a little drier than falafels that are deep-fried in oil, so I always serve them with some kind of sauce. These are just perfect on whole-wheat pasta with tomato sauce, just like real meatballs!

FALAFEL 'MEATBALLS'

320 g/2 cups cooked green or brown lentils, well drained

50 g/½ cup fine rolled oats

70 g/½ cup finely grated carrot or celeriac/celery root (or leftover veggie pulp from juicing)

2 garlic cloves, crushed

1 teaspoon dried oregano

½ teaspoon salt

4 tablespoons plain/all-purpose flour, for rolling

oil, for greasing and brushing

SERVING SUGGESTION
cooked whole-wheat spaghetti

fresh tomato sauce

baking sheet, lined with baking parchment

MAKES 12 'MEATBALLS'

Mix together all the ingredients (except the flour and oil) in a bowl and let sit in the fridge for at least 1 hour, or overnight.

Preheat the oven to 180°C (350°F) Gas 4.

Form the mixture into walnut-sized balls, flatten them slightly and roll in flour, shaking off any excess flour.

Grease the parchment-lined baking sheet with oil and oil each falafel with the help of a silicone brush when you place them on the lined baking sheet.

Bake in the preheated oven for 20 minutes; no need for turning them. They are done when a thin crust is formed and they dry out slightly while getting a golden hue. Serve freshly baked with spaghetti and tomato sauce, but they taste good served the next day, too.

A very basic recipe made of wholegrains and veggies that can be served even to small children – just reduce the amount of spices!

JUICY BROWN RICE FAUX-LAFEL

420 g/3 cups cooked short-grain brown rice (cooked 2:1 water to rice ratio)

70 g/½ cup very finely grated carrot (about 1 carrot)

40 g/½ cup very finely grated celeriac/celery root

80 g/½ cup very finely grated onion (1 small onion)

4 garlic cloves, crushed

40 g/¼ cup finely grated smoked tofu (optional)

2 tablespoons freshly chopped parsley or spring onion/scallion greens

salt, pepper, oregano, chilli/chili powder and sweet paprika, to taste

olive oil, for greasing and brushing

SERVING SUGGESTION

mixed greens

sauce or dip of your choice (see pages 88–103)

baking sheet, lined with baking parchment

MAKES ABOUT 24 SMALL PATTIES

For this dish the rice has to be carefully cooked: it should be neither soggy nor hard. For best results use freshly cooked rice, but, if using leftover rice from the fridge, bring to room temperature first.

Put the cooked rice, grated veggies, garlic, tofu, parsley and some salt, pepper, oregano, chilli powder and paprika in a big bowl. Use your hands to knead the mixture until the ingredients are well combined. Taste and add more salt, pepper, oregano, chilli powder or paprika if needed.

Wet your hands and try to shape a small patty from the mixture – if it is a little sticky and soft, but the patty keeps its shape, it should be ready. Leave the mixture to sit in the fridge for 1 hour, or longer.

Preheat the oven to 180°C (350°F) Gas 4.

Wet your hands and shape about 24 small patties. Grease the parchment-lined baking sheet with oil and oil each falafel with the help of a silicone brush when you place them on the lined baking sheet.

Bake in the preheated oven for 12–16 minutes or until golden and compact with a thin, crunchy crust and a juicy inside. Depending on the oven, you might want to turn them halfway through baking. These are delicious served on a bed of mixed greens and with a sauce or dip of your choice.

These baked falafel have a soft finish and a delicate crust rather than the crispness that comes from deep-frying.

SWEET POTATO FALAFEL

2 medium-sized sweet potatoes (about 350 g/12 oz.)

30 g/½ cup coriander/cilantro leaves and stems

25 g/⅓ cup flat-leaf parsley leaves

2 large spring onions/scallions, roughly chopped

3 garlic cloves, peeled

1 teaspoon ground cumin

1 teaspoon ground coriander

¼ teaspoon cayenne pepper

1 teaspoon baking powder

60 g/½ cup gram flour (chickpea/ garbanzo bean flour)

sesame seeds, to sprinkle (optional)

salt, to taste

TO SERVE

diced cucumber and tomato

thinly sliced red cabbage

roughly chopped flat-leaf parsley

juice of ½ lemon

freshly ground black pepper

Tahini & Cashew Ranch Dressing (see page 114)

pitta breads

a baking sheet, greased with a thin layer of olive oil

MAKES 14–16 FALAFELS

Preheat the oven to 220°C (425°F) Gas 7.

Poke the sweet potatoes with a fork a couple of times and place on the oven rack in the preheated oven. Roast for 40–60 minutes, depending on the size of your sweet potatoes, until soft. Remove from the oven and allow to cool. Once cooled, peel off and discard the skin.

Meanwhile, put the coriander, parsley, large spring onions and garlic into a small food processor and pulse until everything is finely chopped. Alternatively, you can very finely chop these ingredients with a knife.

In a large bowl, mash the sweet potato flesh with a fork, masher or hand-held mixer until smooth. Season with salt, add the spices, baking powder and gram flour and stir vigorously with a rubber spatula or hand-held mixer until everything is well combined. Stir in the herb, onion and garlic mixture until evenly distributed. Let the dough rest in the fridge for 20 minutes.

Preheat the oven again to 200°C (400°F) Gas 6. Scoop out portions of dough with a spoon and then lightly roll into small balls using damp hands to prevent sticking. I go for a size that is somewhere between a ping pong ball and a golf ball. Assemble the falafel on the prepared baking tray and sprinkle with sesame seeds, if using. Bake in the preheated oven for 15–20 minutes until golden on the side touching the tray.

To serve, combine some diced cucumber, tomato, red cabbage and parsley in a bowl with the fresh lemon juice and a little salt and pepper. Serve the falafel with the cucumber-cabbage salad and tahini dressing either in a bowl or packed into a pita bread.

Made with wholesome natural ingredients, this is a fun recipe. To make them gluten-free, use gluten-free oats and make the crumbs using quinoa flakes or gluten-free breadcrumbs. Store them in an airtight container and reheat in the oven or sandwich presser.

CHICKPEA NUGGETS

400-g/14-oz. can chickpeas/ garbanzo beans, drained and rinsed

40 g/⅓ cup rolled/old-fashioned oats

2 tablespoons flaxseeds/linseeds

1–2 tablespoons oat milk

1 teaspoon onion powder

½ teaspoon garlic powder

½ teaspoon dried Italian herbs

salt and freshly ground black pepper

fries and dips of your choice, to serve

CRUMBS

60 g/½ cup wholemeal/ whole-wheat breadcrumbs or quinoa flakes

125 ml/½ cup oat milk

baking sheet, lined with baking parchment

MAKES 15 NUGGETS

Preheat the oven to 190°C (375°F) Gas 5.

Put the chickpeas into a food processor or high-speed blender. Add the oats, flaxseeds, oat milk, onion and garlic powders, dried herbs, and salt and pepper, and pulse to blend until well combined and the chickpeas are finely chopped. Do not over blend.

For the outer crumbs, put the breadcrumbs or quinoa flakes and oat milk into 2 separate small bowls. Shape the chickpea dough into 15 even-size nuggets. Dip each nugget, one at a time, into the milk, then into the breadcrumbs, coating both sides and then put each one onto the prepared baking sheet.

Bake in the preheated oven for 10–15 minutes, turning halfway. Serve hot with fries and dips of your choice.

These reheat well so it's worth making a large batch to enjoy over a few days or for the freezer (defrost before reheating). Serve with brown rice and sliced raw vegetables: cucumbers, cherry tomatoes, carrots and celery. They are also good cold as a sandwich filler, with mayonnaise and some shredded lettuce.

CHICKPEA BITES

1 small onion, coarsely chopped

1 carrot, coarsely chopped

1 celery stick/rib, coarsely chopped

1 garlic clove

2–3 tablespoons extra virgin olive oil or rapeseed/canola oil

400-g/14-oz. can chickpeas/garbanzo beans, drained and rinsed

2 generous tablespoons mayonnaise (or vegan alternative)

2 tablespoons oatbran

1 tablespoon wholemeal/whole-wheat flour

freshly squeezed juice of ½ orange

salt and freshly ground black pepper

plain Greek yogurt, to serve (optional)

non-stick baking sheet, lightly greased

MAKES 12–15 BITES

Preheat the oven to 200°C (400°F) Gas 6.

Put the onion, carrot, celery and garlic in the bowl of a food processor and process until finely chopped.

Heat the oil in a small non-stick frying pan/skillet. When hot, add the vegetable mixture, season with salt and pepper and cook for 3–5 minutes, stirring often until soft. Do not allow the mixture to brown or the garlic will taste bitter. Let cool slightly.

Meanwhile, put the chickpeas, mayonnaise, oatbran, flour and orange juice into the same food processor bowl and process, leaving some small chunks of chickpea; the mixture should not be completely smooth. Transfer the chickpea mixture to a large bowl. Add the vegetable mixture and stir well. Taste and adjust the seasoning.

Form the mixture into walnut-sized balls and arrange on the prepared baking sheet. Bake in the preheated oven for 30–40 minutes until brown and just golden on top. Serve hot, warm or at room temperature with some yogurt on the side if liked.

NO-COOK FALAFELS

A lot of people love falafels, but don't like deep-fried foods, or have difficulty digesting the soaked chickpeas/garbanzo beans that are usually in falafels. Here's a raw and chickpea-free falafel that is surprisingly easy to make, and will fill you up for many hours! Feel free to use whatever seeds you have to hand.

MEDITERRANEAN SEED FALAFEL

120 g/1 cup pumpkin seeds

70 g/½ cup sunflower seeds

60 g/½ cup walnuts

6 sun-dried tomato halves, soaked

50 g/½ cup fresh basil leaves

50 g/½ cup fresh parsley leaves

½ teaspoon dried oregano

½ teaspoon Mediterranean dried herbs mix (thyme, savory, marjoram, rosemary, basil, fennel)

2 garlic cloves, crushed

1–2 tablespoons olive oil

1 tablespoon lemon juice, or to taste

salt

SERVING SUGGESTION

Romaine lettuce leaves

sliced tomato

grated courgettes/zucchini and carrots

sliced spring onions/scallions

Tahini Sauce (see page 113)

MAKES 10–12 FALAFELS

Grind the seeds and walnuts into fine flour (I have a small electric coffee grinder just for this purpose). Chop the tomatoes very finely. Add the chopped tomatoes, together with the remaining ingredients, to the seed flour and mix well with your hands or with a silicone spatula. Wrap in clingfilm/plastic wrap and let sit in the fridge for 30 minutes. (If you are in a hurry, you can skip this and make them right away.)

Pull off portions of the mixture (about the size of small walnuts) and roll into balls.

To serve, put 2–3 falafels on a Romaine lettuce leaf with some tomato, courgette, carrot and spring onions. Top with a drizzle of the tahini sauce or any sauce of your choosing. Roll up like a wrap and munch away!

As the gluten-free movement spreads around the globe, buckwheat has recently seen a rise in popularity. However, there's more to buckwheat than just the fact that it doesn't contain gluten! Since it's technically not a grain, it's much softer than other grains and I use it soaked to make all kinds of raw dishes, including crackers, flatbreads, custard-like creams and, of course, this falafel-style treat for those who prefer uncooked foods.

BUCKWHEAT & CAULIFLOWER BITES

80 g/½ cup buckwheat, soaked overnight, drained well

120 g/1 cup cauliflower florets

½ large onion (about 60 g/2 oz.)

4 sun-dried tomato halves (soaked in hot water, or tapped dry if in oil)

1 tablespoon olive oil

3 tablespoons freshly snipped chives or chopped parsley

½ teaspoon dried thyme

¼–½ teaspoon salt

SERVING SUGGESTION
mixed salad

Super Simple Salsa (see page 109)

avocado slices

dehydrator lined with a tex-flex sheet (or a baking sheet lined with baking parchment)

MAKES 18 BITES

In a small food processor fitted with an 'S' blade, blend the soaked buckwheat until sticky but with some texture left. Scoop the buckwheat into a bowl.

Process the cauliflower and add to the buckwheat. Chop the onion and tomato halves and add to the buckwheat mix along with all the other ingredients. Mix with a spatula to incorporate.

Scoop up a small amount of the falafel mixture and use 2 spoons to shape little oval balls and place them onto the lined dehydrator or baking sheet.

Dehydrate on 60°C (140°F) for 1 hour, lower to 45°C (115°F) and continue dehydrating until the falafels form a crust, with a still slightly moist inside (takes 4–5 additional hours). (Alternatively, use the oven: turn it to the lowest setting, and put in the baking sheet with falafels, wedging the door open with a rolled-up dish towel to prevent overheating.)

Serve with a big salad, simple salsa and slices of avocado. Or however you may fancy!

This is a great example of how natural ingredients combined with the right spices can result in a delicious dish. Drying on low temperature, instead of regular baking, develops an amazingly aromatic taste, especially in recipes with mushrooms.

MUSHROOM & WALNUT FALAFEL

60 g/½ cup walnuts

70 g/1 cup chopped fresh shiitake mushrooms (or other)

½ small courgette/zucchini (about 50 g/2 oz.)

1 garlic clove

small bunch fresh parsley, leaves only

½ small onion (about 40 g/1½ oz.)

2 tablespoons ground flaxseeds/linseeds, or toasted, ground sesame seeds

1 tablespoon tamari soy sauce

1 tablespoon extra virgin olive oil

⅛ teaspoon salt

¼ teaspoon ground ginger

1 teaspoon freshly squeezed lemon juice

SERVING SUGGESTION

plain soy yogurt

spiralized raw vegetables

lemon dressing

dehydrator lined with a tex-flex sheet (or a baking sheet lined with baking parchment)

MAKES 14 FALAFELS

In a food processor fitted with an 'S' blade, separately chop the walnuts, then the mushrooms, then the vegetables (courgette/zucchini, garlic, parsley and onion).

Mix together in a bowl, then add ground flaxseeds or sesame seeds, soy sauce, oil, salt, ginger and lemon juice and combine all the ingredients into a moist paste.

Use a measuring spoon to scoop walnut-sized falafels onto the lined dehydrator or baking sheet.

Dehydrate on 60°C (140°F) for 1 hour, lower to 45°C (115°F) and continue dehydrating until the falafels form a crust, with a still slightly moist inside (takes 4–5 additional hours). (Alternatively, use the oven: turn it to the lowest setting, and put in the baking sheet with falafels, wedging the door open with a rolled-up dish towel to prevent overheating.)

Because this falafel has a strong flavour, I like to eat it with plain chilled soy yogurt and a big bowl of spiralized raw vegetables drizzled with a light lemon dressing. A perfect light lunch that will nourish you without leaving you feeling heavy!

Another falafel-style recipe with nuts as the main ingredient that can be dried in the dehydrator or the oven. You can substitute cashews for soaked sunflower seeds or walnuts, but do not omit the sweet paprika or fresh red (bell) pepper, as both of these give the distinctive flavour and colour to this falafel. These will keep well in the fridge and are a great lunchbox item, too.

PAPRIKA & CASHEW FALAFEL

220 g/2 cups cashews

¼ teaspoon salt, for soaking

70 g/½ cup chopped red (bell) pepper

40 g/¼ cup chopped onion

3 tablespoons freshly chopped parsley leaves

3 teaspoons sweet paprika

½ teaspoon salt

2 tablespoons virgin coconut oil, melted

SERVING SUGGESTION

summer salad with baby spinach leaves, chopped onion and radish

Tahini Sauce (see page 113)

extra seeds, to sprinkle

dehydrator lined with a tex-flex sheet (or a baking sheet lined with baking parchment)

MAKES 18–20 FALAFELS

Put the cashews in a bowl, cover with water, add the ¼ teaspoon salt and let soak for 8 hours or overnight. Discard the soaking water and drain well.

Blend the soaked cashews in a high-speed blender together with the remaining ingredients until smooth.

Use a measuring spoon to scoop walnut-sized falafels onto the lined dehydrator or baking sheet.

Dehydrate on 60°C (140°F) for 1 hour, lower to 45°C (115°F) and continue dehydrating until the falafels form a crust, with a still slightly moist inside (takes 4–5 additional hours). (Alternatively, use the oven: turn it to the lowest setting, and put in the baking sheet with falafels, wedging the door open with a rolled-up dish towel to prevent overheating.)

Serve with a summer salad, tahini sauce and some extra seeds.

These bite-sized falafels are perfect for packing into a lunchbox and go well with any of the dips or sauces in this book. Pack your lunchbox with plenty of fresh salad items and top with these seedy falafels for a nutritious lunch.

PINK SUN-SEED FALAFEL

140 g/1 cup sunflower seeds (raw or slightly sprouted)

2 small carrots (about 60 g/2 oz.)

½ raw beetroot/beet (about 80 g/3 oz.)

35 g/⅓ cup ground flaxseeds/linseeds

grated zest of 1 orange

1 tablespoon freshly squeezed orange juice

2 tablespoons freshly snipped chives

¼ teaspoon ground turmeric

¼ teaspoon ground coriander

2 tablespoons tahini (or toasted, ground sesame seeds)

1 tablespoon olive oil (if using ground sesame seeds instead of tahini)

1 teaspoon umeboshi vinegar (optional)

salt

1 tablespoon raw sesame seeds, for sprinkling

dehydrator lined with a tex-flex sheet (or a baking sheet lined with baking parchment)

MAKES 16 SMALL FALAFELS

In a food processor fitted with an 'S' blade, separately chop the sunflower seeds (you want a slightly chunky consistency), then the carrots with the beetroot/beet. Mix together in a bowl, then add the ground flaxseeds, orange zest and juice, chives, spices, tahini/ground sesame and oil (if using) and combine all the ingredients (except for the raw sesame seeds for sprinkling) into a compact paste.

Form 16 small balls with moist hands, then flatten them slightly. Sprinkle the top of each falafel with raw sesame seeds, and place on the lined dehydrator or baking sheet.

Dehydrate on 60°C (140°F) for 1 hour, lower to 45°C (115°F) and continue dehydrating until the falafels form a crust, with a still slightly moist inside (takes 4–5 additional hours). (Alternatively, use the oven: turn it to the lowest setting, and put in the baking sheet with falafels, wedging the door open with a rolled-up dish towel to prevent overheating.)

Here's a fry-free and chickpea-free falafel that's surprisingly easy to make. It's also a great lunchbox item and the mix can stay fresh in the fridge for days. These green balls go with just about anything – in salads, with cooked vegetables, alongside soups or as an appetizer. It's a great way to introduce more seeds into your diet!

SEED FALAFEL

130 g/1 cup pumpkin seeds

130 g/1 cup sunflower seeds

50 g/½ cup walnuts

5 tablespoons chopped flat-leaf parsley

5 dried tomato halves, soaked

2 garlic cloves, crushed

3 tablespoons olive oil

juice of ½ lemon

1 teaspoon dried oregano

1 tablespoon water, if necessary

salt and freshly ground black pepper

MAKES 24

Grind the seeds in a food processor or blender into a fine flour, making sure you don't process them for too long, otherwise they might turn into seed butter.

Finely chop the walnuts, as they'll give the falafels a nice crunchy texture. Add them, together with the remaining ingredients (except the water) to the seed flour and mix well with your hands or with a silicone spatula. Taste and adjust the seasoning if necessary – it should taste strong and full of flavour. Try squeezing the seed mixture in your hand and if it doesn't fall apart it's moist enough. If it feels dry and crumbles immediately, add the water and mix again.

Form the mixture into walnut-sized falafel balls and either serve them up straight away or keep them refrigerated before use. I find that it's always a good idea to keep a stash of these falafels in the fridge!

MEALS & MORE

This quick and easy dish lets you enjoy the flavours of falafel, without the hassle of frying or the mess of rolling into balls.

UNDONE FALAFEL SALAD

CHICKPEAS/GARBANZO BEANS

2 tablespoons tamari soy sauce

¼ teaspoon chilli/chili powder

¼ teaspoon ground turmeric

¼ teaspoon ground ginger

½ teaspoon ground coriander

¼ teaspoon ground cumin

1 tablespoon olive oil

160 g/1 cup cooked chickpeas/ garbanzo beans, well drained

SALAD

20 g/1 cup rocket/arugula

1 round/butterhead lettuce (about 160 g/5½ oz.)

6 leaves red leaf lettuce

2 ripe tomatoes (about 340 g/¾ lb.)

small bunch of fresh basil

1 portion Mediterranean Seed Falafel mixture (do not form into falafels, see page 50)

2 tablespoons olive oil

2 tablespoons red wine vinegar

Tzatziki (see page 88)

4 pitta pockets, cut into wedges, toasted, to serve

baking sheet, lined with baking parchment

SERVES 2–4

Preheat the oven to 180°C (350°F) Gas 4.

For the chickpeas, mix together all the ingredients apart from the chickpeas to make a marinade. Pour the marinade over the chickpeas and toss to coat well.

Spread the coated chickpeas on the lined baking sheet and bake in the preheated oven until the chickpeas soak in all the marinade and start browning. Alternatively, you could do this in a frying pan/skillet: heat the pan, add the chickpeas, pour over the marinade and mix quickly with 2 wooden spoons over a high heat until fragrant and well roasted.

Wash the salad leaves well and drain. Tear the lettuce leaves into smaller pieces. Cut the tomatoes into wedges and chop the basil. Place all the vegetables in a big wide bowl, crumble over the Mediterranean falafel mixture, add the baked chickpeas and drizzle with olive oil and vinegar. Mix well to incorporate.

Divide between separate plates and serve the tzatziki sauce in 2–4 small bowls, so each person can pour it over the falafel salad just before eating.

A cast-iron pan/skillet is essential for frying these juicy falafel burgers – it means they need very little oil but won't stick to the pan and gives the delicious charred flavour.

CHARRED FALAFEL BURGERS

260 g/1½ cups cooked chickpeas/garbanzo beans, well drained

130 g/¾ cup very finely grated beetroot/beets

130 g/1 cup pre-soaked couscous (pour 120 ml/½ cup boiling water over 65 g/½ cup couscous, add a little salt, cover and let sit for 10 minutes)

70 g/½ cup good-quality bread crumbs

2 tablespoons tahini

3 tablespoons finely chopped onion

2 garlic cloves, crushed

¾ teaspoon salt

½ teaspoon dried thyme

½ teaspoon dried oregano

freshly ground black pepper

sunflower or coconut oil, for frying

SERVING SUGGESTION

6 whole-wheat burger buns

Roasted Red Pepper and Mustard Sauce (see page 110)

lettuce leaves

Tofu Mayonnaise (see page 106)

slices of fresh onion

pickles and wooden barbecue sticks

Super Simple Salsa (see page 109)

MAKES 6 BIG BURGERS

In a food processor fitted with an 'S' blade, pulse the chickpeas. Transfer to a mixing bowl and add all the remaining ingredients, except the frying oil. Use your hands to knead the mixture thoroughly; everything should be well incorporated. Chill in the fridge for 20 minutes, or longer.

Form the mixture into 6 patties. I usually use a big cookie cutter or an American ½ cup measuring cup for one burger – lightly oil the inside to prevent sticking, then fill the cup and turn it over onto a baking sheet. Pat down to make a nicely shaped patty.

Preheat a cast-iron pan/skillet over a medium heat. Pour in 1 tablespoon of oil and add 2–3 patties (more if your pan is bigger). Fry for about 5 minutes each side, adding a tablespoon more oil after the flip. Cook until the patties are heated through, slightly charred and have a thin crust.

This is my serving suggestion for a real burger experience: while the pan is still hot, fry the inside of a whole-wheat bun, spread the bottom part with red pepper and mustard sauce, add lettuce leaves, top with the patty, spread tofu mayo on top, add slices of fresh onion and top with the bun. Pierce with a wooden barbecue stick and add a couple of pickles. Serve with super simple salsa!

It's hard to resist melted cheese in this comforting casserole-style dish! This is something different that everybody will enjoy.

FALAFEL CASSEROLE

230 ml/1 cup tomato sauce (below)

7–9 leftover falafel (choose any from the recipes in this cookbook)

50 g/½ cup grated white cheddar-style vegan cheese that melts well

olive oil, to drizzle

blanched broccoli or any other greens, to serve

toasted sourdough bread or creamy mashed potatoes, to serve

TOMATO SAUCE

(Makes about 375 ml/1½ cups sauce)

3 tablespoons extra virgin olive oil

1 large onion (about 120 g/4 oz.), finely chopped

1 teaspoon vegetable bouillon powder or ½ bouillon cube (optional)

1 teaspoon dried oregano or basil

1 tablespoon rice or maple syrup

1 tablespoon tamari soy sauce

230 ml/1 cup tomato passata

2 garlic cloves, crushed

2 tablespoons freshly chopped parsley or snipped chives

salt and freshly ground black pepper

large baking dish

SERVES 2–3

Start by making the tomato sauce. Heat the olive oil in a pan over a medium heat and sauté the onion until translucent. Add the bouillon powder/cube, herbs, syrup and tamari, and stir until the onion soaks up the spices; about 2 minutes.

Add the passata and bring it to the boil. Now lower the heat and leave to simmer, uncovered, for about 10 minutes, or until thick. At the very end of cooking, add the garlic, parsley or chives and an extra drop of olive oil. Season to taste. This sauce can be made a couple of days in advance and kept refrigerated, if needed.

To assemble the casserole, preheat the oven to 180°C (350°F) Gas 4.

Drizzle a little bit of olive oil in the bottom of the baking dish, pour in the tomato sauce, add a layer of leftover falafel and cover with grated vegan cheese. Bake for 10–15 minutes, until the tomato sauce starts sizzling and the cheese melts. Serve with blanched broccoli or any other greens, and toasted sourdough bread or creamy mashed potatoes.

Chickpea patties add satisfying texture and transform a light vegetable curry into a heartier and more filling meal.

FALAFEL COCONUT CURRY

2 tablespoons virgin coconut oil

1 large onion (about 120 g/ 4½ oz.), finely chopped

1 carrot (about 70 g/ 2½ oz.), chopped into bite-sized pieces

1 celery stick/rib (about 70 g/ 2½ oz.), chopped

2-cm/¾-inch piece of fresh ginger, peeled and finely chopped

2 garlic cloves, chopped

1½ tablespoons mild curry powder

2 teaspoons ground ginger

2 teaspoons ground turmeric

2 teaspoons garam masala

¼ teaspoon chilli/chili powder

2 tablespoons tamari soy sauce

500 ml/2 cups coconut milk (home-made or from carton, not full-fat canned milk)

½ teaspoon salt

leftover Traditional Chickpea Falafels (see page 14) or Red Lentil Falafels (see page 18)

1 tablespoon cornflour/cornstarch, diluted in a little cold water

chopped spring onions/scallions or coriander/cilantro, to garnish

basmati rice, chapatis or toasted pitta pockets, to serve

SERVES 4

Heat the coconut oil in a pan and sauté the onion, carrot and celery with a pinch of salt, until fragrant. Add the ginger, garlic and dry spices, combine and let fry for another minute. Add the soy sauce and stir. Add enough coconut milk to cover the vegetables and bring to the boil, then add the salt, lower the heat and simmer until the vegetables are soft. Add more coconut milk if necessary.

At the end of cooking, add the leftover falafel and diluted thickener of choice (if needed), and let the curry come to the boil one last time. Adjust the seasoning to taste. Garnish with chopped spring onions/scallions or coriander/cilantro and serve with basmati rice, chapatis or toasted pitta pockets.

Bean and veggie patties are always satisfying, but adding tahini to the mix does make them more flavourful as well as more nutrient-dense. Couscous can be substituted with leftover brown rice or other grains.

BEAN & TAHINI BURGERS

120 ml/½ cup boiling water

100 g/½ cup uncooked couscous or 130 g/1 cup cooked couscous

260 g/1½ cups cooked borlotti beans, well drained

130 g/¾ cup very finely grated celeriac/celery root

70 g/½ cup good-quality dried breadcrumbs

4 tablespoons tahini

3 tablespoons finely chopped onion

2 garlic cloves, crushed

¾ teaspoon salt

½ teaspoon dried pizza seasoning

freshly ground black pepper

sunflower oil or coconut oil (melted), for frying

TO SERVE
6 sesame burger buns, tahini, lettuce, tomato slices, coleslaw, onion slices, Tahini Sauce (see page 113)

MAKES 6 BIG BURGERS

Pour the boiling water over the uncooked couscous, add a little salt, cover and leave to soak for 10 minutes. Or use pre-soaked or leftover couscous.

In a food processor fitted with an 'S' blade, pulse the beans. Transfer to a mixing bowl and add all the remaining ingredients, except the frying oil, but including the couscous. Use your hands to knead the mixture thoroughly – everything should be well incorporated. Chill in the fridge for about 20 minutes, or longer. Form into 6 patties. I usually use a 120-ml/½-cup measuring cup for one patty – fill it and then turn over onto a tray. Pat down to make a nicely shaped patty.

Preheat a cast-iron pan over a medium heat. Pour in 1 tablespoon of oil and add 2–3 patties (add more oil and more patties if your pan is bigger). Fry for about 5 minutes on each side, adding another tablespoon of oil after the flip. When ready, the patties should be cooked thoroughly, charred a little and forming a thin crust.

Slice each sesame bun in half and toast. Spread the bottom with tahini, add lettuce and tomato slices, top with a few tablespoons of coleslaw, add the patty then top with onion slices and a drizzle of basic tahini sauce. Top it off with your toasted top bun and you're all set!

This recipe uses a harissa made with rose petals but if you cannot find it, substitute regular harissa paste instead.

MOROCCAN CHICKPEA SOUP WITH FALAFEL & HARISSA POCKETS

3 shallots, finely chopped

15 g/1 tablespoon butter

1 tablespoon olive oil

1 garlic clove, finely sliced

1 teaspoon black onion/nigella seeds

1 teaspoon ground cinnamon

freshly squeezed juice of 2 lemons

1 teaspoon rose harissa

2 x 400-g/14-oz. cans chickpeas, drained and rinsed

80 g/½ cup soft dried apricots

1 litre/quart vegetable stock

freshly ground black pepper

fennel fronds, to garnish (optional)

FALAFEL POCKETS

1 teaspoon rose harissa

200 g/1 cup Greek yogurt (or vegan alternative)

4 wholemeal pitta pockets

12 falafels (choose any from the recipes in this book)

a few handfuls of mixed soft salad leaves

salt and freshly ground black pepper

SERVES 4

For the soup, fry the shallots in the butter and olive oil until they are soft and translucent. Add the garlic and fry until lightly golden brown. Add the black onion/nigella seeds and cinnamon and fry for a minute to heat the spices, stirring all the time. Add the lemon juice, harissa, chickpeas, apricots and stock to the pan and simmer for about 20 minutes. Pour the soup into a blender or food processor and blitz until smooth. Return to the pan and keep warm.

To make the harissa yogurt dressing for the falafel pockets, fold the harissa into the Greek yogurt, season with salt and pepper to your taste, cover and store in the fridge until you are ready to serve.

Warm the pitta breads under the grill/broiler and then cut them open. Fill each with salad leaves and falafel and top with a drizzle of the harissa yogurt dressing.

Pour the soup into bowls and top with chopped fennel fronds, if using, and freshly ground black pepper. Serve straight away with the falafel pockets on the side.

A Middle Eastern-themed dish, packed with spice.

QUINOA TABBOULEH WITH SPINACH FALAFEL

300 g/2 cups dried chickpeas/
garbanzo beans, soaked in cold
water overnight

salt and freshly ground black
pepper

Basic Hummus (see page 91),
to serve

TABBOULEH
170 g/1 cup quinoa

500 ml/2 cups vegetable stock

1 small red onion

100 g/3½ oz. baby plum tomatoes

1 red (bell) pepper

a handful of flat-leaf parsley

freshly squeezed juice of
1 lime

SPINACH FALAFEL
75 g/2½ cups spinach

7 tablespoons olive oil

125 g/1 cup gram flour (chickpea/
garbanzo bean flour)

½ teaspoon chopped red chilli/
chile

SERVES 4

To make the tabbouleh, rinse the quinoa, then place in a pan with the stock. Bring to the boil, simmer for 20 minutes, then turn off the heat and fork through to distribute any remaining stock. This will be absorbed as the quinoa cools.

Drain the chickpeas from their soaking water and rinse. Place in a pan and cover with water. Bring to the boil and cook for at least 30 minutes or until tender. Drain and rinse under cold water to cool.

Complete the tabbouleh by chopping the onion, tomatoes, pepper and parsley. Place in a salad bowl and stir through the quinoa. Squeeze over the lime juice and season to taste. Cover and chill while you prepare the falafel.

To make the falafel, roughly chop the spinach and place in a large bowl. Add the remaining chickpeas, 5 tablespoons of olive oil, the gram flour, chilli, and 2 tablespoons of water and blend with a hand blender. Season to taste. Form into 8 small patties, about 8 cm/3½ inches in diameter and 2 cm/¾ inches thick.

Heat the remaining 2 tablespoons olive oil in a large frying pan/skillet. Add the falafel to the hot oil (you may need to do this in batches). Fry over a medium heat for 5–7 minutes on each side until well browned and hot all the way through.

Serve with the tabbouleh, hummus, lime wedges and extra olive oil, for drizzling.

This mini lunchtime mezze for one is full of lots of different Moroccan-inspired flavours as well as plenty of fruit and veg. There are countless types of ready-made falafel available these days, but if you have time, do make up some of your own.

MOROCCAN MEZZE BOX

250 g/9 oz. falafel (choose any from the recipes in this book)

½ red onion

1 small green (bell) pepper, deseeded

1 cucumber, deseeded

2 tomatoes

3 pitta breads

3 tablespoons extra virgin olive oil

2 tablespoons freshly squeezed lemon juice

1 large carrot, peeled

1 small garlic clove, crushed

a small handful of pomegranate seeds

60 g/⅓ cup natural/plain yogurt (or vegan alternative)

1 teaspoon tahini

2 tablespoons store-bought dukka (a mixture of herbs, nuts, and spices)

MAKES 2 SERVINGS

Cook the falafel following the recipe of your choice and leave to cool.

Finely dice the onion, red pepper, cucumber and tomatoes. Toast one of the pitta breads until really crisp and let cool. Crumble into small pieces. Combine the pitta, diced vegetables, 1 tablespoon of the oil and 1 tablespoon of the lemon juice. Stir well.

Finely grate the carrot and place in a bowl. Add the garlic, pomegranate seeds, remaining oil, lemon juice and some salt and pepper.

Combine the yogurt and tahini in a bowl, then season to taste and stir.

Divide the components into lunchboxes, so that each box contains both salads and the extra pitta breads. Place the tahini yogurt and the dukka in separate small pots, if possible. Seal and chill in the refrigerator until required.

A mezze is a classic Middle Eastern or Eastern Mediterranean way to enjoy falafel, as part of a feast with lots of other small dishes that can be shared. Just add hummus, feta and similarly themed trimmings of your choice.

PUMPKIN-SEED FALAFEL MEZZE

FOR THE BROWN RICE TABBOULEH

340 g/2 cups diced tomatoes

¼ teaspoon salt

2 tablespoons salt-cured capers

320 g/2 cups cooked short-grain brown rice

40 g/1 cup finely chopped fresh flat-leaf parsley

20 g/½ cup finely chopped fresh basil or mint

1½ tablespoon olive oil

2 tablespoons finely chopped onion

2 tablespoons toasted sesame seeds

1 tablespoon apple cider vinegar

freshly ground black pepper

FOR THE PUMPKIN-SEED FALAFEL

(makes 12 balls)

240 g/2 cups pumpkin seeds

6 sun-dried tomato halves, soaked

20 g/½ cup finely chopped fresh basil

20 g/½ cup finely chopped flat parsley

½ teaspoon dried oregano

2 garlic cloves, crushed

1 tablespoon olive oil

1 tablespoon lemon juice, or to taste

¼ teaspoon salt, or to taste

other mezze items of your choice, to serve

SERVES 4

First, make the brown rice tabbouleh. Place the diced tomatoes in a colander, add the salt, mix to combine well and let sit for 15 minutes. Drain all the extra juice away. Wash, drain and chop the capers. Stir all the ingredients together well. Let sit for 1 hour or overnight before serving.

Now, make the pumpkin-seed falafel. Grind the pumpkin seeds into fine flour in a small electric spice grinder or blender. Drain and chop the sun-dried tomatoes very finely. Add the chopped tomatoes to the seed flour together with all the remaining ingredients, and mix well with your hands or with a silicone spatula. Wrap in clingfilm/plastic wrap and let sit in the fridge for 30 minutes. Pull off portions of the mixture (about the size of small walnuts) and roll into balls.

Arrange all of your chosen mezze items, along with the falafels and tabbouleh on a platter to serve.

Evoking the ancient lands, this Levantine-inspired board is full of Middle Eastern and Eastern Mediterranean flavours. Enjoy this with fresh mint tea.

FALAFEL GRAZING BOARD

1 Middle Eastern flatbread (Ramazan pidesi) or 4 pitta breads grilled and cut into fingers

1 red onion, sliced into thin wedges

1 tablespoon sea salt

2 baby cucumbers, halved lengthways

100 g/3½ oz. mixed olives

3 figs, halved (or quartered if large)

1 pomegranate, half seeded, half left intact

100 g/3½ oz. pistachio nuts (in their shells)

8 Medjool dates

FALAFEL

180 g/1 cup dried chickpeas/garbanzo beans

small bunch of fresh coriander/cilantro

small bunch of fresh flat-leaf parsley

1 shallot, chopped

1 garlic clove, chopped

1 tablespoon coriander seeds

1 teaspoon ground coriander

1 teaspoon cumin seeds

1 teaspoon ground cumin

1 teaspoon salt

1 teaspoon baking powder

50 g/⅜ cup sesame seeds

vegetable oil, for deep frying

COFFEE DUKKA SPICE MIX

1 teaspoon fennel seeds

1 teaspoon coriander seeds

1 tablespoon shelled almonds

1 teaspoon sesame seeds

1 teaspoon cumin seeds

1 teaspoon nigella seeds

6 black peppercorns

a pinch of sea salt flakes

½ teaspoon fine ground coffee

TAHINI YOGURT

150 g/¾ cup Greek yogurt (or vegan alternative)

1 tablespoon freshly squeezed lemon juice

a pinch of salt

1 small garlic clove, crushed

1 tablespoon tahini

a pinch of ground cumin

finely chopped fresh flat-leaf parsley

CHARRED AUBERGINE/EGGPLANT SLICES

4 baby aubergines/eggplants, halved lengthways (or sliced 1-cm/½-in. thick if using large ones)

TABBOULEH

50 g/generous ¼ cup bulgur wheat

1 teaspoon tomato purée/paste

½ vegetable stock cube

60 ml/4 tablespoons boiling water

a few sprigs of fresh flat-leaf parsley, coriander/cilantro and mint

1 spring onion/scallion, thinly sliced

1–2 tablespoons pomegranate seeds

salt and freshly ground black pepper

a large round serving plate or platter

SERVES 4–6

FALAFEL

Soak the chickpeas overnight (or ideally for 24 hours) in plenty of water, then drain.

Add the chickpeas with all the ingredients, except the sesame seeds and oil, to a food processor and pulse until you have a fine paste. Take a heaped tablespoon of the mixture and roll into a tight ping-pong ball-sized piece, flatten slightly in the palm of your hand and roll in the sesame seeds. If the falafel do not hold together well, refrigerate for an hour, otherwise continue.

Fill a deep heavy-based pan with vegetable oil, to at least 5 cm/2 inches deep. Heat the oil until a piece of falafel mixture when placed in the oil immediately sizzles but doesn't burn. Fry the falafel pieces for a few minutes until they are crisp and deep golden in colour, then remove using a slotted spoon to drain on paper towels.

Note: You can cheat and use canned chickpeas. If so, add 40 g/heaping ¼ cup plain/all-purpose flour for each 400-g/14-oz. can of chickpeas to hold them together. Not quite as good a texture as the real thing but in a falafel emergency they can work!

COFFEE DUKKA SPICE MIX

Toast everything except the coffee and salt in a dry heavy-based pan for a couple of minutes until you can smell the aroma. Immediately pour the contents into a pestle and mortar or spice grinder along with the salt and bash or pulse to a coarse grain (the almonds will become much more pulverized than the spices). Stir through the coffee and store in an airtight container.

TAHINI YOGURT

Mix all the ingredients together, adding a splash of water if it thickens too much (but you want it quite thick). Pour into a bowl and reserve.

CHARRED AUBERGINE/ EGGPLANT SLICES

Heat a griddle pan to smoking hot and griddle the aubergine slices flesh-side down for 2 minutes until they come away from the pan without sticking and have gorgeous charred lines across them. Griddle the other side for another minute, then brush with a little olive oil and set aside. (You can buy a jar of charred aubergine if preferred.)

TABBOULEH

Rinse the bulgur wheat then place in a bowl with the tomato purée and vegetable stock cube. Pour over the boiling water, mix and cover. Finely chop the parsley and coriander/cilantro including the stalks, remove the mint leaves from the stalks and chop, reserve to one side. After 12 minutes, fluff the bulgur wheat with a fork and fold through the chopped herbs, spring onion/scallion and a tablespoon or two of pomegranate seeds, season with a pinch of salt and pepper and set aside.

HOW TO ASSEMBLE

Start by grouping the larger items around the board; spoon the tabbouleh straight onto the board and add the charred aubergines slices, the falafel (cutting one in half to show off the green hue) and the flatbread or pitta bread in a couple of places.

Spoon the tahini yogurt directly onto the board, drizzling a little olive oil over the top and garnish with a line of dukka across the middle of the yogurt. Cluster the sliced red onions next to little mound of sea salt (for dipping) and add the baby cucumbers. Any remaining areas can be filled with clusters of olives, figs, dates, pomegranates and pistachios.

DIPS

Here's my version of the famous tzatziki dip that is served in every taverna bar on every Greek island, and it's so popular with both natives and tourists!

TZATZIKI

2 cucumbers (about 400 g/ 14 oz.), peeled and grated

500 ml/2 cups soy yogurt

6 tablespoons extra virgin olive oil

1 tablespoon umeboshi vinegar (optional)

2 garlic cloves, crushed

freshly squeezed lemon juice, to taste

1 tablespoon freshly chopped parsley leaves

1 tablespoon freshly snipped chives

salt

MAKES ABOUT 700 ML/3 CUPS

Mix the grated cucumbers with a little salt and let sit for 15 minutes. Squeeze out as much of the cucumber juice as you can, otherwise the liquid will water down the dip.

Mix all other ingredients in a bowl and add the cucumber flesh. Chill until ready to serve.

There you have it! It's the most refreshing snack and it's on my menu every week from the beginning to the end of the cucumber season. A great dip to serve with Greek-style Falafel Fritters (see page 26), but actually, you can also serve it with any other falafel in this cookbook!

This recipe will be a lovely addition to many of the falafel recipes in this book. It is best to cook your own chickpeas, but canned chickpeas can be used too (in this case, just use the cooking water from the can), but keep in mind that the deliciousness of the hummus made with freshly cooked chickpeas puts the bland-tasting versions made with canned chickpeas to shame!

BASIC HUMMUS

320 g/2 cups cooked chickpeas/ garbanzo beans (see pages 10–11), plus 60 ml/¼ cup of the cooking liquid, or more if needed, plus 2 tablespoons cooked chickpeas to serve

2 tablespoons extra virgin olive oil, plus 2 tablespoons to serve

1 tablespoon tahini

3 garlic cloves

freshly squeezed juice of ½ lemon, or to taste

½ teaspoon salt, or to taste

freshly chopped flat-leaf parsley, to garnish (optional)

MAKES ABOUT 2–4 SERVINGS

Blend all the ingredients in a blender or food processor, except the extra chickpeas and olive oil to serve, slowly adding the cooking liquid until you reach a thick and creamy consistency; this will take about 1 minute. High-speed blenders make the creamiest texture and need less liquid and time, but both food processors and stick blenders can be used as well.

Adjust the lemon juice and salt to taste.

Serve topped with 2 tablespoons extra virgin olive oil and 2 tablespoons whole chickpeas. Garnish with chopped flat-leaf parsley, if you like.

Sprouting chickpeas/garbanzo beans is super simple and it transforms the hard seed that takes hours to cook into easier-to-digest quick-cooking sprouts! Blanching them also improves the taste and texture.

SPROUTED CHICKPEA HUMMUS

135 g/¾ cup dried chickpeas/garbanzo beans

1.25 litres/5 cups water

3 tablespoons tahini

2 teaspoons ground cumin

¼ teaspoon smoked paprika, plus extra to garnish

2 garlic cloves

1 tablespoon olive oil

freshly squeezed juice of ½ lemon, or to taste

½ teaspoon salt, or to taste

rice cakes and pickled vegetables (such as radishes, cucumber and red onion), to serve (optional)

MAKES ABOUT 2–3 SERVINGS

Soak the dried chickpeas in water overnight. The next day, drain well, place in a big jar, cover with muslin/cheesecloth and secure with a rubber band. Place in a bowl at a 45° angle, top-down, so that any extra water can easily drain off. Let sprout for 24 hours.

Run cold water through the muslin/cheesecloth to cover the chickpeas, then drain well and place back in a jar. Repeat this for another 24 hours. By now a tiny sprout should already show on top of each seed. I like to sprout for another 24 hours (3 days in total), so each seed has a tail at least half the size of the chickpea itself. Some beans sprout more slowly than others, so adjust your sprouting time. You can store sprouted chickpeas, well drained and air-dried, in a clean jar in the fridge for a couple of days. You should have 300 g/3 cups of sprouts.

For the hummus, bring the water to the boil, add the sprouted chickpeas and cook over a medium heat for 10 minutes. Drain well (saving at least 60 ml/¼ cup of cooking liquid), and let cool slightly.

Blend with all the other ingredients, adding just enough cooking liquid to make a creamy hummus. Adjust the seasoning to taste. Sprinkle with smoked paprika and drizzle with olive oil just before serving. Serve warm or cold. I love spreading it on puffed rice cakes, topped with slices of lightly pickled vegetables – simple yet delicious!

There are never enough greens in our diet! It's especially important not to over-cook the green leafy vegetables, but they can also be used raw, the way I'm using spinach in the following recipe. This way, all the nutrients remain intact and the hummus becomes vibrantly green!

SPINACH HUMMUS

**320 g/2 cup cooked chickpeas/
garbanzo beans (see pages 10–11),
plus 60 ml/¼ cup of the cooking
liquid, or more if needed**

3 tablespoons extra virgin olive oil

1 tablespoon cashew butter

3 garlic cloves

**1 tablespoon umeboshi vinegar
(not essential, but adds gusto)**

70 g/1 handful raw spinach leaves

**freshly squeezed juice of ½ lemon,
or to taste**

½ teaspoon salt, or to taste

**freshly chopped flat-leaf parsley,
to garnish (optional)**

**Vegetable Crisps/Chips (see page
154), to serve (optional)**

MAKES ABOUT 2–3 SERVINGS

Blend all the ingredients in a blender or food processor, slowly adding the cooking liquid until you reach a thick and creamy consistency; this will take about 1 minute. (High-speed blenders make the creamiest texture and need less liquid and time, but both food processors and stick blenders can be used as well.)

Adjust the lemon juice and salt to taste. Garnish with chopped flat-leaf parsley, if you like, and serve with vegetable crisps/chips for dipping.

The earthy intense sweetness of baked beetroot/beets adds a deep, rich flavour to this hummus.

PURPLE BEETROOT HUMMUS

2 beetroot/beets, well washed, with skin

1 quantity Basic Hummus (see page 91)

1 teaspoon caraway seeds

salt

olive oil, for drizzling

baking sheet lined with baking parchment

SERVES 2–4

Preheat the oven to 200°C (400°F) Gas 6.

Rub a pinch of salt into the beetroot. Wrap them well in foil. Place on the lined baking sheet and bake in the preheated oven for about 45 minutes, or until the beetroot flesh is soft. Let cool slightly. Peel, discard the skins and tops and blend in a blender or food processor into a smooth purée.

Blend the beetroot purée into the creamy hummus a little at a time (reserving a little to swirl in at the end if, you like). It should be done slowly until the desired consistency, colour and taste are reached. Taste and adjust the seasoning. Stir through the caraway seeds or sprinkle on top. Swirl through any reserved beetroot purée and drizzle with extra olive oil to serve, if you like.

This hummus is packed full of Mediterranean flavours. I usually bake garlic bulbs once a week, then squeeze out the flesh and keep it in an airtight container in the fridge to use in different recipes.

MEDITERRANEAN TOMATO HUMMUS

1 garlic bulb

10 sun-dried tomato halves

320 g/2 cups cooked chickpeas/garbanzo beans (see pages 10–11), plus 60 ml/¼ cup of the cooking liquid, or more if needed

1 tablespoon tahini

3 tablespoons extra virgin olive oil (2 for the hummus and 1 to serve)

bunch of fresh basil, chopped, plus a few whole leaves to garnish

1 sprig of thyme, leaves only

3 tablespoons chopped parsley leaves

2 teaspoons lemon juice

½ teaspoon salt, or to taste

¼ teaspoon dried rosemary powder

freshly ground black pepper

coarse sea salt and 1 teaspoon olive oil, for baking the garlic

MAKES ABOUT 2–3 SERVINGS

Preheat the oven to 180°C (350°F) Gas 4.

Brush the garlic head with oil, rub in some coarse sea salt, wrap in aluminium foil and bake for 40 minutes or until the garlic flesh becomes soft. Use half of the amount in this recipe and save the remaining paste to add to other dishes.

Soak the sun-dried tomato halves in warm water for 30 minutes. Drain and discard the soaking water. (If using oil-packed tomato halves, there's no need to soak them, but omit 2 tablespoons of olive oil in the recipe, since the tomatoes will bring enough oil to the hummus.) Chop finely.

Blend the chickpeas with the tahini, slowly adding the cooking liquid, until it has reached the desired consistency. Spoon it out into a bigger bowl and stir in the chopped tomato halves, half the garlic bulb paste, chopped basil, the thyme leaves, 2 tablespoons of the olive oil, 2 tablespoons of the chopped parsley, the lemon juice, salt and freshly ground black pepper to taste. Sprinkle with the dried rosemary powder and the remaining chopped parsley, and garnish with the whole basil leaves and a drizzle of olive oil.

This is a fresh alternative to traditional hummus. The nutty flavour of broad/fava beans works really well with lemon and the sesame of the tahini.

BROAD BEAN HUMMUS

300 g/2½ cups fresh broad/fava beans

400-g/14-oz. can chickpeas/garbanzo beans, drained and rinsed

50 g/¼ cup tahini

2 roasted garlic cloves (see Note)

grated zest and freshly squeezed juice of 1 lemon

salt and freshly ground black pepper

toasted bread, to serve

SERVES 4

Put the broad beans in a saucepan of cold, unsalted water and set over a medium heat. Bring to a low simmer and continue to simmer for 5 minutes. Drain, then put in a bowl of cold water and chill in the fridge to halt the cooking. After a few minutes, remove the outer skins and discard, reserving the inner beans to use in the hummus.

Put the beans and the remaining ingredients in a large mixing bowl with ½ teaspoon of salt. Blend to a fine paste using a handheld electric blender. Taste the mixture and add extra salt if needed. Sprinkle with black pepper and serve right away with toasted bread or cover and store in the fridge for up to 4 days.

Note: To roast garlic, place a whole bulb of garlic on a baking sheet and cook in a preheated oven at 180°C (350°F) Gas 4 for 45 minutes. You can easily do this while you're cooking something else and save it in the fridge until you need it. You will now have a bulb of soft garlic paste that can be squeezed, like a tube of toothpaste, one clove at a time.

A great take-away snack or a quick lunch, paired with homemade crackers, rice cakes or freshly baked bread, and a side salad.

WALNUT TAHINI HUMMUS

200 g/1½ cups walnuts, soaked for at least 4 hours and well drained, plus extra (chopped) to serve

80 g/⅓ cup tahini

60 ml/¼ cup extra virgin olive oil, plus extra to serve

60 ml/¼ cup freshly squeezed lemon juice, or to taste

¾ teaspoon salt, or to taste

1½ teaspoons crushed cumin seeds or 1 teaspoon ground cumin

2 garlic cloves

freshly ground black pepper

freshly chopped parsley, to serve

MAKES 370 G/1½ CUPS

In a food processor fitted with an 'S' blade or in a high-speed blender, blend all the ingredients together, adding 120 ml/½ cup water until you reach a creamy texture. Taste and adjust the seasoning.

Serve drizzled with a little extra olive oil and scattered with chopped walnuts and chopped herbs.

SAUCES, DRESSINGS & PICKLES

If you love yogurt-based sauces, but are avoiding dairy and soy, then here's a great alternative! Cashews are mild in taste and can be used as a base in many delicious recipes, especially those mimicking yogurt or cream cheese dishes.

CASHEW 'YOGURT' SAUCE

180 g/1⅓ cups cashews

4 tablespoons freshly squeezed lemon juice, or to taste

1 teaspoon agave syrup (optional)

MAKES ABOUT 400 ML/1⅔ CUPS

Put the cashews in a bowl, cover with water and let soak for 24 hours. Drain, discarding the soaking water and rinse well.

Blend the soaked cashews with the rest of the ingredients and 175 ml/¾ cup cold water in a high-speed blender until silky smooth. Keep refrigerated and use within 2 days.

A vegan version of popular mayonnaise that is much lighter and much less oily than regular mayo, or even the store-bought vegan versions. This pairs up very well with any falafel.

TOFU MAYONNAISE

300 g/2 cups fresh tofu

60 ml/¼ cup olive or sunflower oil

3 tablespoons freshly squeezed lemon juice or apple cider vinegar

1 soft pitted/stoned date

½ teaspoon sea salt

MAKES ABOUT 240 ML/1 CUP

Blend all the ingredients together with 90 ml/⅓ cup water until completely smooth.

Taste and adjust the seasonings. I like it tangier so I always add a little more lemon juice or vinegar. Also, pay attention to what you will serve it with; if used as a salad dressing, it needs to be more sour, and if used with salty foods like falafel, make it less salty.

Apart from using avocado for guacamole or sliced in salads, it can be blended into a creamy dip that goes well with everything.

HERB & AVOCADO DIP

1 ripe avocado (about 250 g/ 9 oz.), peeled and stoned/pitted

4 tablespoons olive oil

1 tablespoon tahini

1 tablespoon freshly squeezed lemon juice

1 teaspoon tamari soy sauce

¼ teaspoon cayenne pepper, or to taste

bunch of fresh herbs (basil, coriander/cilantro, parsley, lemon balm/melissa)

coconut milk or water, as needed

salt

MAKES ABOUT 240 ML/1 CUP

Place the avocado in a blender or food processor, add all the other ingredients and blend until smooth, adding coconut milk or water until the desired consistency. Taste and adjust the seasoning.

Note: You can use any nut/seed butter instead of tahini – peanut butter, for example, is an interesting choice. You can make endless variations of this dip/sauce by adding garlic, onion or vinegar – all depending on what you have in the pantry. Lemon juice postpones the browning process of the avocado, but even so, it's best used the same day.

This fresh and herby pesto goes perfectly with falafels.

CORIANDER-FETA PESTO

60 g/3½ cups coriander/cilantro, chopped

50 g/⅓ cup walnuts, chopped

100 g/3½ oz. feta (or vegan alternative), crumbled

80 ml/⅓ cup olive oil

MAKES ABOUT 240 ML/1 CUP

In a food processor, blitz the coriander/cilantro, walnuts and feta into a chunky mixture, then add the olive oil. Mix in the oil, keeping the texture of the pesto chunky.

With fried foods such as falafel, it's very important to serve raw vegetables alongside to add nutrition. This easy salsa tastes even better the next day!

SUPER SIMPLE SALSA

3 ripe tomatoes (about 550 g/ 1¼ lbs.), stems removed

a handful of fresh basil leaves

3 tablespoons finely chopped onion

1 garlic clove, finely chopped

3 tablespoons extra virgin olive oil

¼ teaspoon dried oregano

salt and freshly ground black pepper

MAKES ABOUT 700 ML/3 CUPS

Slice the tomatoes in half and remove the juice and the seeds. Dice the flesh and place in a serving bowl. Tear the basil leaves by hand and add them to the tomatoes together with all the other ingredients. Mix well and let sit for at least half an hour to allow the flavours to combine.

The best variety of peppers to use for this yummy sauce are long, red pointed Romano peppers, but if you can't find them you can use red (bell) peppers too. Roasting peppers deepens their flavour and gives a wonderful aroma, and goes well with any kind of falafel.

ROASTED RED PEPPER & MUSTARD SAUCE

1 kg/2¼ lbs. Romano peppers

60 ml/¼ cup extra virgin olive oil

2 tablespoons smooth Dijon mustard

4 garlic cloves, crushed

apple cider vinegar, to taste

chilli/chili powder or freshly ground black pepper (optional)

sea salt

baking sheet, lined with baking parchment

MAKES ABOUT 240 ML/ 1 CUP

Preheat the oven to 180°C (350°F) Gas 4.

Wash and pat-dry the peppers, leaving them whole. Place the whole peppers on the baking sheet and roast in the preheated oven for 20–25 minutes, turning frequently until the entire pepper skin has turned black and blistery.

Remove from the oven, put the peppers into an airtight container and let rest, tightly covered for long enough to build up some steam; about 15 minutes. This will make peeling the skins easier.

Save all the liquid that leaks from the peppers while cooling, then peel and deseed them, saving the liquid coming out as you do so.

Blend the peeled and deseeded peppers in a blender or food processor until smooth, adding the oil, collected juices, Dijon mustard, garlic, salt and a little vinegar. You can also add a little chilli powder or black pepper, for extra heat. Add more pepper juice or oil to reach the desired consistency. Store in a tightly covered sterilized jar in the fridge and use within 1 month.

Buying tahini is really easy and there are lots of good-quality brands out there, but there's just something very satisfactory in making it at home, from scratch. It's definitely cheaper, too. You just need to invest a bit of time and energy in it, and owning a high-speed blender is really helpful if you want it to turn out oily and creamy, as it should be.

TAHINI SAUCE

4 tablespoons tahini (see below)

1 garlic clove, crushed

1 tablespoon freshly snipped chives

freshly squeezed lemon juice, to taste

about 120 ml/½ cup oat, rice or almond milk

salt and freshly ground black pepper

TAHINI

450 g/3 cups unhulled sesame seeds

¼ teaspoon salt

MAKES ABOUT 150 ML/⅔ CUP

Start by making the paste. Place the sesame seeds in a very fine-mesh sieve/strainer and wash thoroughly under running water. Do not skip this step, as the sesame seeds will toast much more evenly and washing them prevents them from jumping out of the pan. Drain really well.

Put the sesame seeds in a cast-iron frying pan/skillet over a medium heat. Roast in 2 batches, if the whole amount doesn't fit in the frying pan/skillet at once. Dry-roast the seeds, stirring constantly until the seeds turn golden brown and start puffing up and cracking. Check if they are done by placing a couple of seeds between your fingers – if the seeds crumble easily, they are ready.

Blend the seeds in a high-speed blender with the salt, pushing them down from the sides with the tamper while blending. After a couple of minutes, the ground sesame seeds will start turning into a creamy tahini! Spoon out into a sterilized dry jar, let cool and keep tightly covered.

To make the tahini sauce, mix together the tahini, garlic, chives, lemon juice and a little salt and freshly ground black pepper, adding just enough milk to get a smooth sauce. Refrigerate any leftovers for later use.

Try this vegan alternative to a regular ranch dressing. It can be used not only for dressing salads but also as a dip for crudités or as a spread in sandwiches.

TAHINI & CASHEW RANCH DRESSING

130 g/½ cup tahini

60 g/½ cup cashews, soaked in cold water for 4 hours, drained and rinsed

130 g/½ cup vegan mayonnaise

2 tablespoons apple cider vinegar, or to taste

2 garlic cloves

1 tablespoon Dijon mustard

½ teaspoon salt

10 g/¼ cup freshly chopped dill and chives, plus extra to serve

freshly ground black pepper

MAKES 320 ML/1⅓ CUPS

Using a blender, blend the tahini, cashews, mayonnaise, vinegar, garlic, mustard and salt, slowly adding cold water to reach the desired consistency. Transfer to a bowl and fold in the chopped herbs and pepper to taste. Taste and adjust the vinegar and/or salt, to taste. Cover and keep refrigerated for up to 4 days.

An interesting combo of tastes: pungent ginger, sweet carrot and slightly bitter tahini.

CARROT & GINGER DRESSING

100 g/1 large carrot, chopped

70 g/1 small onion, chopped

2-cm/¾-inch piece of fresh ginger, peeled

2 tablespoons parsley greens

2 soft dates, pitted

2 tablespoons tahini

2 tablespoons soy or oat cream

1 tablespoon umeboshi vinegar or salt to taste

1 tablespoon apple cider vinegar, or to taste

MAKES 320 ML/1⅓ CUPS

Using a blender, blend all the ingredients together with 120 ml/½ cup cold water into a smooth dressing. Store in a sealed jar in the fridge for up to a week.

A simple dressing with the addition of tahini that can be made ahead and stored in a sealed jar in the fridge for a couple of days.

SIMPLE TAHINI VINAIGRETTE

4 tablespoons tahini

12 tablespoons apple cider vinegar, or to taste

grated zest and freshly squeezed juice of 2 lemons

4 tablespoons tamari soy sauce

15 g/½ cup finely chopped parsley greens

water, as needed

salt and freshly ground black pepper

**MAKES 415–480 ML/
1¾–2 CUPS**

Whisk all the ingredients together in a bowl until the tahini is dissolved. Taste and adjust the seasoning. It should taste quite strong and a bit on the salty side to complement the mild taste of raw salad and vegetables.

Three of my favourite ways to give leftover hummus a chance to feel good about itself again, all dressed up as a salad dressing.

HUMMUS SALAD DRESSINGS

CAPER-INFUSED HUMMUS DRESSING

80 g/⅓ cup leftover hummus

2 teaspoons salt-cured capers

1 tablespoon olive oil

a handful of fresh basil

1 tablespoon freshly squeezed lemon juice

60 ml/¼ cup water

MAKES ABOUT 150 ML/⅔ CUP

SMOKY HUMMUS DRESSING

80 g/⅓ cup leftover hummus

3 tablespoons chopped onion

1 teaspoon smoked paprika

½ teaspoon sweet paprika

1 tablespoon sunflower oil

¼ teaspoon salt

1 tablespoon apple cider vinegar

60 ml/¼ cup water

freshly ground black pepper

MAKES ABOUT 150 ML/⅔ CUP

GARLICKY HUMMUS DRESSING

80 g/⅓ cup leftover hummus

2–3 garlic cloves

¼ teaspoon salt

1 tablespoon olive oil

1 tablespoon freshly squeezed lemon juice, or to taste

½ teaspoon ground turmeric

60 ml/¼ cup soy or oat creamer

MAKES ABOUT 150 ML/⅔ CUP

For each recipe, simply blend all the ingredients in a food processor or blender into a smooth and creamy dressing.

Any vegan mayonnaise can be turned into a dressing simply by adding more liquid and blending it in. This type of dressing goes well with almost anything, and the fact that it contains nuts and seeds (and all of the good oils that they possess) makes it very satisfying. Use in salads, sandwiches or as a dip for falafels or raw vegetables.

CASHEW MAYONNAISE DRESSING

90 g/⅔ cup unsalted cashews

85 g/⅔ cup sunflower seeds

3 tablespoon olive oil

¾ teaspoon sea salt

1 soft stoned/pitted date

180 ml/¾ cup cold water

1 tablespoon lemon juice

2 garlic cloves (optional)

MAKES 400 G/1⅓ CUPS

Soak the nuts and seeds overnight, drain, discard the liquid and rinse.

Put the soaked nuts and seeds in the blender with all other ingredients and blend until completely smooth – only a high-speed blender can achieve the velvety smoothness needed for this dressing! If it's too thick, add more water to reach the desired consistency.

Cover and let sit at room temperature for 6–8 hours to ferment a bit more and to allow the flavours to develop.

This is just one of many variations of kimchi. Pickling at home is often neglected and people do not realize how important it is for good digestion to eat naturally fermented foods on a daily basis. You can always have a couple of jars in different stages of fermentation in your pantry and take a spoonful or two every day with your main meal – it's that easy! It's worth making plenty at once and using it up in 30–60 days.

HOME-FERMENTED KIMCHI

1.2 litres/5 cups water

3 tablespoons sea salt

600 g/7 cups julienned green cabbage

180 g/2½ cups chopped leeks

10 g/a handful of dulse seaweed

20 g/¾ oz. piece of fresh ginger, peeled

4 garlic cloves

1 teaspoon ground turmeric

1 whole medium-sized chilli/chile pepper

pickle press (optional)

MAKES 12–15 SERVINGS

Make a brine by mixing the water and salt and stirring well until the salt dissolves. Put the cabbage and leeks into a pickle press and cover with the brine. To keep them submerged, screw the lid down just a little. Allow to soak for a few hours, or overnight if possible. If you don't have a pickle press, put the vegetables in a bowl and weigh them down by resting a plate on top of them.

In the meantime, crush the ginger and garlic. Soak the seaweed in cold water for 30 minutes, drain and finely chop.

Drain the soaked vegetables, but be sure to keep the brine. Mix the turmeric in with the vegetables, seaweed, crushed ginger and garlic and add the chilli pepper.

Put this mixture back into the pickle press or bowl and add enough brine to rise over the veggies once you press them down. Screw the lid down as much as you can, or, if using a plate, put something heavy on top of it. Allow to ferment for a minimum of a week. The best taste develops after 4 weeks!

Many different types of fermenting and pickling can be found under the name turshiya throughout the Balkans and the Middle East but this version uses natural fermentation.

TURSHIYA *(mixed vegetables in brine)*

1 small cauliflower (about 480 g/
17 oz. in weight)

8 small carrots (about 220 g/
8 oz. total weight)

4 small onions (about
320 g/11½ oz. total weight)

4 green Babura peppers or other
sweet (bell) peppers (about
400 g/14 oz. total weight)

2 cucumbers (about 450 g/1 lb.
total weight)

120 g/½ cup sea salt

3-litre/quart pickle press

7-litre/7½-quart crock, bucket
or similar

**MAKES 1 X 7-LITRE/7½-QUART
JAR, CROCK OR BUCKET**

Wash the vegetables (do not scrub them too hard, though, because this removes enzymes beneficial for fermentation) and remove any dark spots. Remove any leaves from the cauliflower and break it into fairly large florets. Leave the carrots whole or slice them lengthwise. Peel the onions and cut into quarters. Slice the peppers in half lengthwise, remove the stem and seeds and cut each half again lengthwise into 2–3 slices. Cut the cucumbers into thick half-moons, with the skin on. Place all the vegetables into the crock or bucket.

In a separate bowl, whisk together 3 litres/quarts water with the salt until dissolved. Pour over the vegetables.

Find a plate or lid that fits into the crock or bucket and place over the vegetables to keep them submerged in the brine at all times. Use a small stone to keep the lid from floating, if necessary. It is not necessary to create pressure to make turshiya. Cover with a clean dish towel and let sit at room temperature, but away from direct sunlight. The fermentation process will start in about 2 days with some foam forming on the surface of the liquid. Check the crock or bucket every 2–3 days, remove any mould that might appear and continue fermenting. Depending on the room temperature the vegetables can be ready in 3–4 weeks, but in colder temperatures it can take up to 2 months. Be patient, check your crock or bucket frequently and taste the vegetables from time to time to see how the flavour is developing. After they are sour to your taste, pack them in clean jars, cover in the brine and keep refrigerated.

These salad pickles can be made the day before eating, or they can be stored in a jar in the refrigerator for up to 2 weeks. Pickles and preserves are generally served as a starter in Marrakesh alongside other salads, or they are enjoyed as a snack with savoury pastries, brochettes or merguez sausages. They can really be made with any vegetables you have to hand.

MIXED SALAD PICKLES

2 medium carrots, peeled and cut into matchsticks

1–2 white radishes, peeled and cut into matchsticks

1 small cucumber, peeled, deseeded and cut into matchsticks

1 red (bell) pepper, deseeded and cut into matchsticks

a few generous pinches of sea salt

2 tablespoons blanched almonds

2 teaspoons pink peppercorns

1–2 teaspoons cumin seeds

a pinch of saffron fronds

1–2 cinnamon sticks

freshly squeezed juice of 2–3 lemons

1 tablespoon white vinegar

2 tablespoons sugar

1–2 tablespoons orange flower water

small bunch of fresh coriander/cilantro, finely chopped

SERVES 4–6

Put all the vegetables in a bowl and sprinkle with the salt. Leave to weep for 30 minutes, then rinse and drain well.

Tip the vegetables back into the bowl and add the almonds, peppercorns, cumin seeds, saffron and cinnamon sticks. Add the lemon juice, vinegar and sugar and mix well. Cover the bowl and chill for 6 hours, or overnight.

Before serving, stir in the orange flower water and coriander. Serve the pickles at room temperature.

This is a wonderful way to ferment late spring and summer vegetables and fruits and use up any spare yogurt/kefir. Ripe fruit gives a nice sweet kick to this salsa. Instead of cherries you could use a ripe mango, apricot, peach or plum.

CULTURED SALSA CRUDA

1 cucumber (about 220 g/ 8 oz. in weight)

2 ripe tomatoes (about 340 g/ 12 oz. total weight)

2 onions (about 140 g/5 oz. total weight)

25 g/½ cup sliced spring onion/ scallion greens, chopped parsley or dill

freshly squeezed juice of 1 lemon

1 mild fresh chilli/chile pepper

70 g/½ cup ripe cherries, stoned/ pitted

20 g/1 generous tablespoon Himalayan pink salt (fine grain), or other salt

960 g/4 cups yogurt whey (see opposite) or water

2-litre/quart glass jar with tightly fitting lid

MAKES 1 x 2-LITRE/QUART JAR

Peel the cucumber if it hasn't been organically grown. Chop all the vegetables and put in a big bowl. Add the lemon juice, sliced chilli pepper and the cherries. Whisk the salt and yogurt whey together well in the jar, then add the bowl contents and mix well. Close tightly and let sit at room temperature for up to 10 days – in summer it will be ready after around 4 days.

Open the lid a couple of times during the day because carbon dioxide, which is the by-product of fermentation, builds up inside the jar. Alternatively, don't close the lid tightly at all; however, the end product will be less fizzy. When the vegetables are sour to your taste, keep them in the fridge and eat up the salsa within a month. A spoonful or two of cultured salsa cruda is a great condiment with any meal and can also be added to your everyday salad. It's very refreshing!

How to make yogurt whey: Put a large sieve/strainer over a large bowl. Place a straining bag in the sieve and pour 1.2 litres/5 cups yogurt (or vegan yogurt) into the bag. Fold the top of the bag so that the yogurt cannot leak out, cover with something heavy (a bowl or measuring weight) and allow the whey to drain off for 8–12 hours, or longer. Use the cream cheese left in the straining bag for other recipes, and the strained whey here.

PITTAS, FLATBREADS & CRACKERS

Making good pitta breads at home is just a matter of following a well-tested recipe – and having enough patience to knead the dough for 10 minutes!

PITTA BREAD

STARTER

80 ml/⅓ cup lukewarm water

2 teaspoons maple sugar or another sweetener

9 g/1 tablespoon active dry yeast

DOUGH

400 g/3¼ cup plain/all-purpose flour, plus extra for dusting

100 g/¾ cup wholemeal/ whole-wheat flour

1½ teaspoons sea salt

2 tablespoons olive oil, plus extra for oiling

270 ml/1 cup plus 2 tablespoons lukewarm water

dough scraper (optional)

baking sheet, lined with baking parchment

MAKES 10 PITTAS

Whisk together the starter ingredients and rest, covered with a damp towel, in the oven with the light on for 30 minutes or until slightly bubbly.

In a large bowl, whisk together the flours and salt for the dough. Add the water, oil and the starter and mix in with a wooden spoon. Knead the dough, first inside the bowl, then on a clean surface for 10 minutes. Don't add extra flour – the dough should be sticky but will come together eventually. Using a dough scraper helps initially.

Oil the bowl and the dough, place the dough in the bowl, cover with a damp towel and let rise in the oven, with the oven light on, for 3 hours or until doubled in size – even better if you make the dough a day ahead and let it rise in the fridge overnight.

Preheat the oven to its maximum (usually 250°C (475°F) Gas 9) and choose the 'lower heat element with fan' setting if you can. Weigh out about 10 small 80-g/3-oz. portions of dough, place on a floured surface and let rise for another 10 minutes.

On a floured surface, gently roll each ball into a 15-cm/6-inch circle. Use a spatula to flip them over as you put them on the lined baking sheet, so the floured side is on top. Four should fit on one sheet.

Open the preheated oven and slide the baking paper with the pittas directly onto the bottom of the oven, without the tray. Bake for 5 minutes until puffed up and lightly browned on the bottom. Open the oven, slide the baking paper with done pittas back onto the baking sheet and repeat with the remaining dough. Wrap in a clean dish towel until ready to serve. Freeze any leftovers.

This is a great hummus-dipper, especially for Indian-spiced hummus. In case you're avoiding yeasty breads, chapatis are a great alternative, and so easy to make!

CHAPATIS

150 g/1 cup wholemeal/
whole-wheat flour, plus extra
for dusting

150 g/1 cup plain/all-purpose
flour, plus extra for dusting

½ teaspoon sea salt

140 ml/generous ½ cup
lukewarm water

2 tablespoons sesame or olive oil

**MAKES 10 CHAPATIS,
13 CM/5 INCHES IN DIAMETER**

Put both flours in a bowl. Add the salt and oil, and whisk to combine. Gradually add the water and knead to form a smooth, medium-soft dough. Kneading is crucial, so do not skip this step and continue kneading until you get the right consistency (depending on the flours you're using, you might need to add a bit more flour or water). Wrap in clingfilm/plastic wrap and set aside for 15 minutes to rest.

Divide the dough into 10 equal portions and form each portion into a ball, rolling them until smooth and without cracks. Coat each ball in flour and roll out them out into chapatis, 13 cm/5 inches in diameter, with the help of a rolling pin. Lightly coat each chapati in flour on both sides to prevent from sticking.

Heat a cast-iron or stainless-steel pan over a medium heat and start frying. The chapati is ready for turning when bumps appear on its surface, but it shouldn't brown. Turn it onto the other side and flip again once the bumps appear. After the second flip, leave it in the pan for a moment, and then gently press the chapati around its edges with a dish towel or oven mitt. It should puff up in the middle! Continue with the remaining chapatis. Serve immediately or cover with a dish towel to prevent drying out.

The ingredients for these crackers might sound a bit weird, since I'm not adding any flour, and raw veggies go directly into the dough, but please give this recipe a chance and you'll discover how healthy ingredients can also make delicious crackers! Great choice as a hummus dipper if health-conscious foodies are coming over for a snack.

RED PEPPER & BUCKWHEAT CRACKERS

270 g/1½ cups buckwheat, soaked in water overnight and well drained

5 tablespoons flaxseeds/linseeds or chia seeds, soaked in water, plus 1–2 tablespoons extra for sprinkling

½ teaspoon sea salt

100 g/1 medium red (bell) pepper

60 g/½ cup chopped onion

1 tablespoon sweet paprika

¼ teaspoon smoked sweet paprika, plus extra for sprinkling

110 ml/½ cup pure carrot juice or water

MAKES 12–16 CRACKERS

In a high-speed blender blend all the ingredients into a thick paste. Use a tamper to push down the mixture to get a smooth texture.

Cut a piece of baking parchment to the size of your oven rack/baking pan and place it on a smooth surface (kitchen counter or table). Spoon the cracker paste onto the baking parchment and spread to get a rectangle-shaped even surface. If you like really crunchy crackers, the dough should be almost paper-thin, but if you like a bit of texture, roll to desired thickness. Sprinkle the dough evenly with extra soaked flax or chia seeds and a couple of pinches of smoked sweet paprika. Put the oven rack/baking pan on the edge of the counter and quickly pull the baking parchment with the cracker paste to slide onto it.

Place in the top of the oven; turn on the fan and the heat up to 100°C (200°F). Prop the door open with a folded dish towel, to ensure proper dehydration. Dehydrate for 2–3 hours.

Check the cracker dough and, if it isn't sticky, peel off the baking parchment and break into your desired shapes. Further dehydrate the crackers directly on the oven rack until dried. If you have a dehydrator, use it – you know what you have to do! Store in a ziplock bag in the fridge.

Grissini are delicious on their own, but pairing them with hummus for a snack or a nutritious appetizer is a great idea, especially if sesame seeds are added into the grissini dough! That way, even if there was no tahini in the house for the hummus, you still get a kick of sesame!

SESAME GRISSINI

140 ml /²⁄₃ cup lukewarm water

5 g/scant 2 teaspoons active dry yeast

5 g /1 teaspoon barley malt (or agave syrup)

190 g /1½ cups plain/all-purpose flour

60 g/½ cup wholemeal/whole-wheat flour

4 g/scant 1 teaspoon salt

2 tablespoons raw, unhulled sesame seeds, plus 1 tablespoon extra for sprinkling

3 tablespoons light sesame or olive oil

2 baking sheets, lined with baking parchment

MAKES 20 GRISSINI (ABOUT 35 CM/14 INCHES LONG)

In a small bowl, combine the water with the yeast and malt. Whisk and let sit for 15 minutes for the yeast will start to foam lightly.

In a separate bowl, combine the flours, salt, sesame seeds and 2 tablespoons of the oil. Stir in the bubbly yeast mixture and knead until smooth; about 4 minutes. Place on a lined baking sheet. With the help of a silicone spatula, oil the dough lightly. Let rise in the oven with only the light on, for 1 hour.

Preheat the oven to 180°C (350°F) Gas 4.

Form the dough into an oval shape and, with the help of a sharp wide knife, cut 1-cm/³⁄₈-inch strips of dough. Stretch each strip with your fingers into a long grissino; some strips will be longer and thicker, so you'll be able to stretch 2 or 3 grissini out of them. From this amount of dough, you should get 20 grissini (35 cm/14 inches long and 1 cm/³⁄₈ inch thick). They do puff a little while baking. I never use a rolling pin to stretch them since that flattens them and pushes out the air, which results in tough grissini.

Place the stretched grissini on the second lined baking sheet, 7 mm/¼ inch apart. Brush with the remaining oil and sprinkle with the extra sesame seeds. Bake in the preheated oven for 12–15 minutes in two batches, rotating them halfway through. Let cool and, if any are left, store in a sealable bag.

This dough takes a bit of time, but it's so worth the wait! No one can resist the delicious smell of freshly baked focaccia.

CARAWAY SEED FOCCACCIA BREAD

STARTER

40 g/¼ cup rye flour

55 ml/¼ cup lukewarm water

9 g/1 tablespoon active dry yeast

DOUGH

200 g/1½ cups unbleached spelt flour, plus extra for kneading

30 g/¼ cup wholemeal/ whole-wheat flour

4 g/scant 1 teaspoon salt

110 ml/½ cup lukewarm water

1 tablespoon olive oil, plus extra for drizzling

1 tablespoon soy milk

2–3 teaspoons of caraway seeds (or fennel seeds or dried oregano)

1 teaspoon coarse sea salt

23 x 30-cm/9 x 12-inch baking pan, well oiled

MAKES 1 LOAF

Mix together the starter ingredients, cover and let sit for 30 minutes.

Mix the flours and salt in one bowl and mix the water, olive oil and soy milk in another bowl. Add the liquids to the starter, incorporate well and then gradually add the flour mixture. Mix the dough with a wooden spoon, and then knead on a floured surface for 5 minutes, or longer, until soft and slightly sticky. Add flour as you knead, but not more than necessary. Place in a big oiled bowl, and oil the surface of the dough, too. Cover with a wet cloth and let rise for 2½ hours in a warm place.

Once risen, shape the dough to fi t the oiled baking pan by gently pressing down from the centre towards the edges. Make dimples by poking the dough with your fingertips. Drizzle with olive oil, cover and let rise again for 2 hours. Do not skip this step, as the end result will be much tougher without this second rising.

Preheat the oven to 180°C (350°F) Gas 4.

Sprinkle the dough with the dried caraway seeds and coarse salt. Bake in the preheated oven for 20 minutes, or until golden and crisp. Let cool slightly before cutting.

Focaccia sandwiches are exceptionally popular with my family and friends – I cut 1 focaccia into 6 equal pieces, cut them in half lengthwise, spread hummus on the bottom half, top that with falafel, and add as many vegetables, pickles, sprouts and greens as I can fit inside. It's a complete meal in itself, very nutritious and very filling!

This is a fantastic way to prepare and serve polenta, with the polenta turning delightfully creamy if it is left to soak in water. Any spices can be added, so feel free to experiment! Once cooled, the polenta is cut into thick slices and grilled/broiled before serving, for an additional smoky aroma. You can also skip this step and serve it without grilling/broiling.

GRILLED CORN CAKE

170 g/1 cup polenta/coarse cornmeal

¾ teaspoon sea salt

½ teaspoon sweet paprika

½ teaspoon dried oregano

4 tablespoons olive oil, plus extra for grilling/broiling

450-g/1-lb. loaf pan

MAKES 1 X 450-G/1-LB. LOAF

Soak the polenta in 600 ml/2½ cups water for about 48 hours. You'll know that it's fermenting when small bubbles start to appear. At this point, pour in a heavy-bottomed saucepan and bring to a slow boil, whisking vigorously. Add salt, paprika and oregano and stir for a bit longer. Lower the heat to a minimum, cover and let sit for 10 minutes. Remove from the heat, cover, and allow to sit for another 10 minutes before stirring well and adding the olive oil.

Oil the loaf pan – the size of the pan isn't that important since you can simply spoon polenta in one corner if the loaf pan is too big. Add the polenta and even out with a spatula or moist hands. The 'loaf' should be 5–6 cm/2–2½ inches thick. Let cool completely, then turn out to a clean work surface. With a sharp wet knife, carefully cut 1-cm/⅜-inch thick slices. Brush each slice with olive oil on both sides and place under a hot grill/broiler; it's best when charcoal or a gas grill is used, but a grill pan works too. Serve instead of bread or as an accompaniment to falafel or a mezze selection.

One of many variations of a simple yeast-free bread I've been making for decades. Instead of the usual addition of oil, I'm adding tahini, and the gram flour (chickpea/garbanzo bean flour) makes this bread wonderfully protein-rich.

TAHINI BREAD

60 g/¼ cup tahini

240 ml/1 cup sparkling mineral water

240 ml/1 cup kefir or soy yogurt (or vegan alternative)

330 g/2¾ cups spelt flour

130 g/1 cup gram flour (chickpea/garbanzo bean flour)

2 teaspoons aluminium-free baking powder

1½ teaspoons salt

4 tablespoons raw unhulled sesame seeds

450-g/1-lb. loaf pan lined with baking parchment (to fit inside without any creases)

oven thermometer (optional)

MAKES ABOUT 14 SLICES

Preheat the oven to 220°C (425°F) Gas 7.

Whisk together the tahini, sparkling water and kefir or soy yogurt in a mixing bowl until dissolved. Sift the flours, baking powder and salt directly into the wet ingredients.

Stir vigorously with a spatula until it reaches a smooth, thick batter consistency.

Sprinkle 2 tablespoons of the sesame seeds onto the bottom of the prepared loaf pan and then spoon in the dough, making sure that it is level. Sprinkle with the remaining sesame seeds and press lightly with your fingers. Put the pan into the preheated oven. Lower the temperature to 200°C (400°F) Gas 6 and bake for 1 hour. Use an oven thermometer if you're not sure about the exact temperature in the oven. If the temperature is below 200°C (400°F) Gas 6, the bread will not rise properly.

Remove the loaf pan from the oven, tip the bread out immediately, peel off the paper and allow to cool completely on a wire rack. This will prevent the bread from absorbing moisture and will keep the crust crisp. Wrap the bread in a clean dish towel and store in a cool, dry place for up to 4 days. Serve in slices.

You can either use these crackers as a dip after they've cooled down, or you can spread them with hummus, then top that with falafels and raw or fermented veggies and munch away!

RYE CRACKERS WITH CHIA SEEDS

130 g/¾ cup rye flour

130 g/¾ cup plain/all-purpose flour

15 g/2 tablespoons chia seeds

4 g/scant 1 teaspoon salt

freshly ground black pepper

60 ml/¼ cup olive oil or light sesame oil

60 ml/¼ cup water

1 teaspoon dark agave or maple syrup

hummus, cucumber and micro cress, to serve (optional)

baking sheet, lined with baking parchment

MAKES 12–16 CRACKERS

Combine all the dry ingredients in a large bowl. Emulsify all the wet ingredients with a whisk, and then slowly add them to the flour and seed mixture, stirring until well combined. The dough should quickly form a ball and shouldn't be sticky. Knead a couple of times; just enough to make sure all the ingredients are evenly distributed. Wrap in clingfilm/plastic wrap and let sit at room temperature for 10 minutes. Resting the dough makes rolling it out much easier.

Preheat the oven to 200°C (400°F) Gas 6.

Divide the dough into 3 equal pieces. Roll out a very thin layer of dough between 2 sheets of baking parchment. If you like really crunchy crackers, the dough should be almost paper-thin, but if you prefer a bit of texture instead, roll to desired thickness.

Use a knife or pizza cutter to cut out shapes. Squares or rectangles are practical choices, since you'll have not much leftover dough. Transfer the crackers to the lined baking sheet using a thin spatula or a knife. Prick each a couple of times with a fork.

Bake for 4–7 minutes, depending on the thickness of the crackers. Remember, they shouldn't brown, just get slightly golden. They will firm up as they cool, so don't expect them to be cracker-crunchy straight out of the oven.

Here, they are spread with hummus and topped with cucumber and micro cress, but you can eat them how you prefer! Store in an air-tight container after they've cooled completely.

Buckwheat is a really healthy seed that is often overlooked, but I think it's a big shame not to eat it from time to time! Try these crackers as a snack topped with a chutney or roasted vegetables.

BUCKWHEAT CRACKERS

95 g /½ cup buckwheat

85 g /⅔ cup sunflower seeds

100 g/1 cup grated vegetables or leftover pulp

¾ teaspoon sea salt

1 medium red (bell) pepper, seeded

60 g/½ cup diced onion

½ teaspoon dried oregano

¼ teaspoon dried thyme

¼ teaspoon dried basil

2 tablespoons ground flaxseeds/ linseeds

3 tablespoons olive oil

110 ml/½ cup vegetable juice or water

40 x 32-cm/16 x 12½-inch wire rack or baking pan

MAKES 15

Preheat the oven to 80°C (175°F) or the very lowest setting.

In a high-speed blender, mix all the ingredients into a thick paste. Cut a piece of baking parchment to the size of your oven shelf/rack or baking pan and place it on a smooth surface. Spoon the paste so that it's about 3-mm/⅛-inch thick onto the parchment paper in a large rectangle. Put the oven rack/baking pan on the edge of your kitchen counter and quickly pull the baking parchment to slide it on. Place the oven shelf/rack or baking pan in the upper part of the oven; turn the heat up to 100°C (210°F), but prop the door open with a folded dish towel, to ensure proper dehydration of the buckwheat. Dehydrate for 2–3 hours.

Peel off the baking parchment, and use a pizza cutter to cut the crackers into the desired shape; dehydrate the crackers directly on the oven shelf/rack for another 30 minutes if you want them really crispy. I love them a bit on the soft side, but dry crackers last longer without spoiling.

Gluten-free crackers are great to have on hand if you want to avoid eating a lot of bread or store-bought crackers. I always have a stash in my cupboard and make a double amount since they keep for over a month, if dried/baked well.

BUCKWHEAT & TAHINI CRACKERS

80 g/⅓ cup tahini

90 g/½ cup buckwheat

90 g/⅔ cup sunflower seeds, plus extra, for sprinkling (optional)

100 g/1 cup grated celery

¾ teaspoon salt

1 green (bell) pepper, deseeded

2 spring onions/scallions

2 tablespoons ground flaxseeds/ linseeds

1 teaspoon flaxseeds/linseeds, for sprinkling (optional)

110 ml/⅓ cup plus 2 tablespoons celery juice or water

MAKES 20–24 CRACKERS

Preheat the oven to 80°C (175°F) or the very lowest setting.

In a high-speed blender blend all the ingredients into a thick paste. Cut a piece of baking parchment into the size of your oven rack/baking pan and place it on a smooth surface (kitchen counter or table). Spoon the cracker paste onto the baking parchment and spread very thinly into a rectangular shape with an even surface. Put the oven rack/baking pan on the edge of the counter and quickly pull the baking parchment to slide onto it.

Sprinkle the paste with the extra sunflower seeds and the flaxseeds/linseeds, if using.

Place in the upper part of the preheated oven and increase the temperature to 100°C (225°F) Gas ¼. Prop the oven door open with a folded dish towel, to ensure proper dehydration. Dehydrate for 2–3 hours.

Remove from the oven and peel off the baking parchment. Use a pizza cutter to cut into desired shapes or break into pieces, then return the crackers to the oven and dehydrate directly on the oven rack/baking pan for another 30 minutes if you want them totally crispy. I love them a bit on the soft side, but dry crackers last longer without spoiling. Use instead of bread or as a really healthy snack.

These are a perfect crisp and savoury cracker for dipping in any of the hummus recipes in this book.

RYE & TAHINI CRACKERS

130 g/1 cup rye flour

130 g/1 cup plain/all-purpose flour

2 tablespoons black or unhulled sesame seeds

½ teaspoon salt

freshly ground black pepper

60 g/¼ cup tahini

1 teaspoon brown rice syrup

baking sheet, lined with baking parchment

MAKES ABOUT 16

Mix together the flours, seeds, salt and some pepper in a bowl. In a separate bowl, whisk the tahini and syrup with 60 ml/¼ cup water to emulsify. Slowly pour into the bowl of dry ingredients, stirring until well combined. The dough should quickly form a ball and shouldn't be sticky. Knead a couple of times, just enough to make sure all the ingredients are evenly distributed. Wrap the dough in clingfilm/plastic wrap and allow to rest at room temperature for 10 minutes. This will make rolling out the dough much easier. Divide the dough into 3 equal portions. Preheat the oven to 200°C (400°F) Gas 6.

Place the dough between sheets of baking parchment and use a rolling pin to roll it out very thinly. For really crunchy crackers, the dough should be almost paper-thin, but if you like a bit of texture, roll it to your preferred thickness. Use a knife or a pizza cutter to cut out shapes; squares or rectangles are most practical, as you'll have hardly any leftover dough. Re-roll any trimmings. Transfer the crackers to the prepared baking sheet using a spatula or thin knife. Prick each one a couple of times with a fork.

Bake in the preheated oven for 4–7 minutes, depending on the thickness of the crackers. Remember that they shouldn't brown, just get slightly golden. They will firm up as they cool, so don't expect them to be cracker-crunchy straight out of the oven! Allow to cool completely and store in an airtight container for 1–2 weeks.

Who doesn't like using regular potato crisps/chips as a hummus dipper? These make a great addition to any falafel mezze spread (see page 83) or just as a perfect light snack on their own. Do not expect them to be as crunchy as deep-fried crisps, but their amazingly rich taste will compensate for that.

VEGETABLE CRISPS/CHIPS

400 g/3 large carrots

400 g/2 large beetroots/beets (you can use regular or a mix of golden or candied)

400 g/3 large parsnips

3 tablespoons olive oil

1 teaspoon fine sea salt

MAKES ABOUT 4-6 SERVINGS

Scrub all the root vegetables well and remove the tops and any black spots. Using a mandoline, slice them lengthways to get the longest strips possible. Small pieces will shrink into bite-size crisps/chips. Also, the slices should not be see-through thin.

Place in separate bowls and add 1 tablespoon of oil and ⅓ teaspoon salt to each batch. Mix thoroughly.

Place on dehydrator trays in a single layer and dehydrate for 2 hours on maximum temperature, then lower the temperature to 50°C/100°F and dehydrate for another 5 hours, or until crispy.

I prefer making tortilla chips without adding any other type of flour except for the finely ground yellow cornmeal, because I love the taste and the texture, and it also means they are gluten-free! However, these tortilla chips have to be eaten soon after baking, since they turn pretty hard and chewy after they cool down completely. Substitute half of the amount of cornmeal with wheat or spelt flour if you want them to keep well for longer.

HOMEMADE CORN TORTILLA CHIPS

150 g/1 cup finely ground yellow cornmeal

½ teaspoon sea salt, or to taste

1 tablespoon sesame seeds

1 tablespoon olive oil

240 ml/1 cup boiling water

MAKES 20–24 TRIANGLE-SHAPED CHIPS

Preheat the oven to 150°C (300°F) Gas 2.

In a bowl, combine the finely ground yellow cornmeal, salt and sesame seeds. Whisk, then add the oil and boiling water. Stir until well incorporated; you should get a soft dough, but not sticky.

Cut 2 pieces of baking parchment to the size of your baking sheet. Place one paper on the work surface and top with the dough, then top the dough with the second paper. Use a rolling pin to roll out the dough to about 1 mm/1/16 inch thick.

Bake in the preheated oven for 10 minutes. Take out and mark with a knife into triangle shapes, or shapes of your choice. Continue baking for another 7–10 minutes, just until the dough stops being soft. Overbaking will make the chips too hard, so be careful! Let cool and break into the marked shapes. Serve the same day with one of the hummus recipes in this book or a falafel mezze spread.

INDEX

RECIPE CREDITS

All recipes are by Dunja Gulin except:

GHILLIE BASAN
Mixed Salad Pickles

MATT FOLLAS
Broad Bean Hummus

KATHY KORDALIS
Coriander-feta Pesto
Grainy Falafel

THEO A. MICHAELS
A Taste of the Levant

HANNAH MILES
Moroccan Chickpea Soup with Falafel &
Harissa Pockets

LOUISE PICKFORD
Moroccan Mezze Box

CLAIRE POWER
Chickpea Nuggets

LEAH VANDERVELDT
Sweet Potato Falafel

LAURA WASHBURN-HUTTON
Chickpea Bites

SARAH WILKINSON
Quinoa Tabbouleh with Spinach Falafel

PICTURE CREDITS

TIM ATKINS
Pages 1, 2–3, 5, 7, 9, 15, 16, 19, 20, 23, 24, 26–7,
28–9, 35, 36, 39, 40, 51, 52, 55, 56, 59, 65, 66,
69, 70, 88–9, 107, 109, 111, 112.

PETER CASSIDY
Pages 126.

MOWIE KAY
Pages 10, 31, 81, 82–5, 90, 93, 94, 97, 98, 118,
133, 134, 137, 138, 141, 146, 155, 156.

ADRIAN LAWRENCE
Pages 77.

STEVE PAINTER
Pages 74, 101.

WILLIAM REAVELL
Pages 60, 122, 149.

TOBY SCOTT
Pages 121, 125, 129, 142.

KATE WHITTAKER
Pages 47.

CLARE WINFIELD
Pages 43, 44, 73, 102, 114, 116–7, 145, 150, 152.